AF557810

Freedom on Trial

'The history of India's freedom struggle is incomplete without the many trials of its freedom fighters—proceedings that captured the imagination of the public and offered these remarkable individuals a powerful platform to place their radical ideas before the nation. Today, these trials are often reduced to passing footnotes. I am glad that writer-lawyer Akash Vajpai has retold them in a way that vividly brings out their drama and significance. A must-read for anyone who wants to understand the individuals and ideas that ultimately led to India's Independence.'

—Sanjeev Sanyal
Bestselling Author and Economist

'This book by Advocate Akash Vajpai is a timely read and forms part of the larger corpus of literature being produced in Bharat that takes a relook at Bharat's history through a refreshingly new lens. The USP of this book is that it examines Bharat's movement for independence through the eyes of a trained lawyer, bringing to the fore twelve trials that bear testimony to the courage and resistance of individuals who powered the movement. Naturally, this book will be of interest to history aficionados, lay readers, students of law, and legal practitioners alike, for different reasons. I would strongly recommend engaging with this book to understand the confrontation between the colonial justice system and Bharat's quest for *swarajya*.'

—J. Sai Deepak
Senior Advocate, Supreme Court of India, and Author

'This book takes the reader back to a time when some of India's bravest sons stood in the dock as accused, only to be vindicated by the verdict of history. Going beyond a mere account of trials, it reflects on courage, conscience, and unwavering conviction. A scholarly, impressive, and compelling work by advocate and author Akash Vajpai.'

—Mukul Rohatgi
Senior Advocate and former Attorney General for India

'*Freedom on Trial* powerfully recounts some of the most iconic pre-Independence trials that shook the foundations of the British Empire. From Mangal Pandey to Bhagat Singh, from Savarkar to Gandhi, and many others, the book brings together the courtroom battles of India's greatest freedom fighters. These trials became platforms where ideals were boldly asserted and national consciousness was awakened. Advocate and author Akash Vajpai skilfully simplifies complex legal proceedings, making these historic cases accessible to a wide readership. An engaging and compelling read.'

—Chetan Sharma
Senior Advocate and Additional Solicitor General of India

Freedom on Trial

Twelve Cases That Shaped India's Struggle for Independence

Akash Vajpai

RUPA

Published by
Rupa Publications India Pvt. Ltd 2026
161-B/4, Gulmohar House,
Yusuf Sarai Community Centre,
New Delhi 110049

Sales centres:
Bengaluru Chennai
Hyderabad Kolkata Mumbai

P-ISBN: 978-93-7646-915-4
E-ISBN: 978-93-7646-725-9

First impression 2026

10 9 8 7 6 5 4 3 2 1

Printed in India

This book is dedicated to my
parents and first teachers,
Deepak Bajpai and Krishna Bajpai,
who taught me to speak, to think, to write,
and, above all, to be human.

CONTENTS

Appendices

FOREWORD

In *Freedom on Trial*, Akash Vajpai revisits a recurring truth of constitutional history—that some trials endure not for the verdicts they delivered, but for the questions they posed, questions that continue to resist closure long after the courtroom has fallen silent. They belong to a formative moment when law was asked to perform tasks for which it was never morally equipped—to secure obedience rather than justice, to preserve authority rather than legitimacy. Yet, even as instruments of a colonial state, these trials became sites where constitutional ideas were first rehearsed, not in statutes or assemblies, but in acts of resistance, reasoned defiance, and moral courage. To engage with them today is to recognize that the constitutional project did not begin in 1950; it was forged earlier, in courtrooms where liberty had no textual guarantee, but possessed an undeniable ethical force.

What lends these trials their enduring relevance is the clarity with which they expose the distance between legality and justice. The colonial courts often functioned with a veneer of procedural correctness and doctrinal certainty. Charges were framed with precision; evidence was marshalled; sentences were imposed ostensibly, in faithful obedience to the law as it then stood. The outcomes serve as enduring reminders that legality, when detached from moral purpose, can transform into an efficient instrument of injustice. These proceedings compel us to confront an uncomfortable truth—that a legal system may be internally coherent and externally oppressive at the same time. The value of revisiting these trials lies in this disquieting lesson that fidelity to law cannot be reduced to technical compliance with the forms of the law.

For a constitutional democracy, institutional memory performs a vital role. Courts do not operate in historical isolation; they inherit traditions, habits of reasoning, and assumptions about power. The trials documented here form part of that inheritance. They remind us of a time when dissent was prosecuted as disloyalty, when political beliefs were recast as criminal intent, and when the courtroom was used to discipline conscience. Understanding this past is essential not to pass retrospective judgment, but to cultivate institutional humility. It sharpens our awareness of how easily law can be bent to serve dominant power, and how vigilant constitutional institutions must remain to prevent that recurrence.

These trials also matter because they shed light on the origins of our constitutional commitment to liberty, equality, and dignity. The freedoms enshrined in Part III of the Constitution are not abstract ideals; they are answers to lived histories of suppression and struggle. Each prosecution chronicled in this book underscores why protections for free expression, fair trial, and personal liberty were made non-negotiable. In that sense, these trials are not relics of a closed past. They are continuing conversations, reminding judges, lawyers, and citizens alike that the legitimacy of law ultimately rests not in its authority to punish, but in its capacity to do justice.

Law, Legality, and Moral Blindness

This tension between law's authority and justice's demands calls for a more searching inquiry into the circumstances in which fidelity to legal form can nonetheless become complicit in injustice. Law, legality, and moral blindness are not a contradiction in terms, but a recurring pattern in constitutional history. Law is not always morality in procedural dress. The colonial state mastered a form of legalism that was meticulous in method and indifferent in conscience. Charges were drafted with precision, evidence was tendered with formality, judgments were pronounced with austere confidence. Quills were broken in solemn subservience to the commands of a colonial state. The moral blindness lay elsewhere—in the premise that the sovereign's security was the highest public good, and that political aspiration, when voiced outside the permitted script, was a pathology to be punished. The trials in this book expose that central contradiction. They show a system capable of administering law, while being unmoored from justice.

These proceedings also reveal a deeper truth about *rule by law*. A regime may speak through statutes and courts, and still remain authoritarian in spirit. Colonial criminal law did not operate merely as a neutral set of prohibitions. It functioned as a grammar of subordination, one that converted political opposition into offences against authority, organized public anger into the legal architecture of conspiracy, and translated moral protest into penal guilt. The sedition provision, so often invoked in that era, illustrates this logic with particular sharpness: when the state collapses itself into the nation, criticism ceases to be speech and is treated instead as hostility. Mahatma Gandhi's prosecution for sedition in 1922, where the law was turned against the most public expression of conscience, was not an aberration. It was a method.

This is the point at which the author's historical narration opens a jurisprudential window for our own time. Constitutional democracy does not ask courts to abandon legality; it asks them to see legality whole, its text, its purpose, its consequences. A legal system that is faithful only to technical form can become blind to the injuries it authorizes. Indian free speech jurisprudence has repeatedly cautioned against this danger by recognizing the *chilling effect*, understanding that coercive law can silence speech not only through conviction, but also through the pervasive fear of its invocation, when fear becomes the citizen's first response to public participation. The Supreme Court's articulation of chilling effect in *Shreya Singhal* was grounded in precisely this insight—that censorship can be *insidious* when the law's shadow grows longer than its lawful aims.

Sedition jurisprudence provides an equally instructive illustration of legality struggling to find its moral limits. *Kedar Nath Singh* upheld Section 124A while reading it down to offences involving incitement to violence or public disorder. The decision recognized that mere criticism, even if sharply worded, cannot be criminalized in a constitutional order. The doctrinal move was significant—it was an attempt to place conscience back into the interpretation of coercive power by insisting upon a nexus between speech and public disorder. The ongoing debate around sedition, evident in subsequent proceedings, reveals how fragile that settlement can be when political impatience seeks legal language for silencing opponents.

Contemporary constitutional practice has also offered an institutional response to this history. The Supreme Court's order of 11 May 2022 in *S.G. Vombatkere v. Union of India*, directing that the use of Section 124A be kept in abeyance while the Union reconsidered the provision, reflected a judicial awareness that colonial inheritances require heightened constitutional scrutiny in a living democracy. It was, at its core, a recognition that the legitimacy of a penal law depends not only on its presence in a statute book, but also on its compatibility with constitutional commitments in the present tense. That posture matters when one reads the freedom trials chronicled in this volume—it shows how a constitutional court can acknowledge history without being imprisoned by it.

The phrase *moral blindness* acquires a deeper, institutional resonance when viewed against the experience of the Emergency. That period forced Indian constitutionalism to confront an unsettling question—whether courts, in moments of profound democratic stress, may come to mistake formal authority for constitutional principle. The judgment in *ADM Jabalpur* endures in public memory not merely as an outcome, but as a cautionary moment in which formal authority and legality were permitted to displace the constitutional protection of liberty. Its significance lies less in the failings of individuals than in the structural vulnerability of legal systems to confuse obedience to power with fidelity to law.

Constitutional democracies mature not by denying such moments, but by engaging them with honesty. The ability of an institution to look inward, to acknowledge error, and to recover its foundational commitments is itself a measure of constitutional strength. Indian constitutional law has, over time, undertaken that difficult task. The explicit overruling of *ADM Jabalpur in Justice K.S. Puttaswamy* marked more than a doctrinal correction; it was an affirmation that the

Constitution does not permit liberty to be suspended at the altar of expediency, and that fundamental rights are not gifts of the state, but restraints upon it.

Reflection on that episode also underscores a broader institutional responsibility. Constitutional adjudication does not end with the delivery of judgment; it carries with it a continuing obligation to interrogate the assumptions that shaped past decisions. When courts confront moments in which constitutional principle was compromised, the task is neither denial nor defensiveness, but honest engagement. The willingness of an institution to acknowledge error and recalibrate its understanding of liberty is integral to the integrity of constitutional governance. Judicial legacy, in this sense, is not something to be preserved intact, but rather something to be tested against the enduring values of the Constitution, requiring courts, like the societies they serve, to retain the capacity to learn, especially from their own mistakes.

What emerges from this arc is a deeper understanding of judging itself. Courts do not preserve their legitimacy through claims of infallibility. They earn it through the courage to correct course when constitutional essentials have been compromised. The willingness to acknowledge error is not a weakness of the judicial institution; it is one of its moral resources. Constitutional adjudication, in that sense, is not a static exercise in authority. It is a continuing ethical practice, one that demands humility, intellectual honesty, and an unwavering commitment to human dignity.

The freedom trials examined in this book reveal how moral blindness often disguises itself as legal order. Colonial courts rarely perceived themselves as unjust. Their procedures were intact; their doctrines were settled; their authority was unquestioned. The blindness lay in the assumption that the legality of power supplied its legitimacy. In that world, the law's role was not to mediate between authority and liberty, but to secure obedience. The accused were not merely individuals on trial; they were embodiments of a political claim the law refused to recognize.

Reading these proceedings today underscores how a legal system may operate with internal coherence while remaining ethically impoverished. The charge of sedition, the language of conspiracy, and the insistence on allegiance to an imperial sovereign functioned as a closed grammar, one that denied moral agency to those who stood before the court. The result was a jurisprudence that could not hear conscience when it spoke in the vocabulary of dissent. These trials, therefore, expose a fundamental lesson—legality, when insulated from moral scrutiny, risks becoming a mechanism of erasure.

That blindness was not accidental; it was produced through method. Colonial adjudication narrowed the frame of inquiry so severely that larger questions of justice were rendered legally irrelevant. Once the court defined its task as enforcing allegiance rather than examining legitimacy, the outcome became inevitable. The law's categories—*sedition, war against the Crown, and criminal conspiracy*—were treated as self-evident, immune from interrogation. Moral choice was translated into criminal intent, and political imagination was recast as unlawful will. This method of reasoning allowed the court to remain procedurally exact while being substantively detached from the realities it judged. In that detachment lies the danger—when law refuses to ask why power is claimed, it ends up asking only whether it has been disobeyed.

The book's narratives also demonstrate how, even within

that constricted legal universe, a counter-ethic struggled to surface. Defence arguments invoking conscience, political self-determination, or the legitimacy of resistance did not always succeed in law. Their significance lay elsewhere. They forced the courtroom to confront questions it was institutionally reluctant to answer. In that sense, these trials were early rehearsals of constitutional reasoning, conducted before a Constitution existed. They anticipated a future in which the law would be required to justify itself not merely by authority, but by reason.

That anticipation finds resonance in the Constitution's insistence on reason-giving as a discipline of power. Modern constitutional adjudication demands that restrictions on liberty be justified by purpose, proportionality, and necessity. The discipline of reason-giving is not ornamental; it is a safeguard against moral blindness. It compels the state to explain why power must be exercised, who it burdens, and whether less intrusive alternatives exist. The colonial prosecutions chronicled here failed precisely because they were indifferent to these questions. They treated political opposition as a pathology rather than a form of participation.

Judicial independence acquires meaning in this context not as insulation from criticism, but as openness to principle. Courts preserve their legitimacy when they recognize that law must be accountable to constitutional values, not merely to precedent or power. These trials remind us of the costs of forgetting this truth. They also illuminate why constitutional adjudication must resist the temptation to treat national security, public order, or sovereignty as talismanic phrases. Each invocation must be tested, justified, and critically reviewed. Absent the discipline of constitutional scrutiny and reasoned justification, the language of necessity risks becoming a means through which injustice is clothed in legality.

This history places a particular responsibility on contemporary courts. The constitutional promise is not fulfilled by distance from the past, but by attentiveness to it. The errors of colonial legality were not committed in ignorance; they were committed in confidence. Awareness of that confidence should instil caution in the present. The task of judging, as these trials remind us, is not to perfect authority, but to restrain it. Law serves democracy best when it remembers that its highest loyalty is owed not to power, but to the dignity of those who stand before it.

The Author's Method—Letting Trials Speak for Themselves

What distinguishes this work is not the force of its commentary, but the discipline of its restraint. The author resists the familiar temptation to impose a single interpretive frame upon events that were themselves fractured, contested, and unresolved. The archive is allowed to breathe. Courtroom exchanges, procedural turns, and the cadence of legal argument are presented with a quiet fidelity that trusts the intelligence of the reader. Meaning emerges not through instruction, but through encounter.

This method reflects an ethical choice in writing about historical events. Trials are not treated as vehicles for verdicts retrospectively supplied, but as moments suspended in uncertainty, where outcomes were shaped by power, persuasion, fear, and conviction in unequal measure. By preserving that uncertainty, the narrative restores agency to those who stood before the law, whether as accused, counsel, or judge. The reader is invited into the position of a listener, not an adjudicator, attentive to what the record discloses and what it withholds.

Such an approach has a particular value for constitutional culture. It reminds us that law is not only a system of answers, but a practice of listening. When history is narrated without haste to resolve it, the past resists closure and continues to question the present. By allowing the trials to speak largely in their own voice, the author achieves something rare—a history that does not instruct, yet endures, precisely because it refuses to conclude.

Courts, Conscience, and the Verdict of History

Seen from that perspective, courts pronounce judgments within the constraints of their time. History, by contrast, is unburdened by immediacy. It does not sit in appeal over findings of fact or doctrine, yet it renders a verdict of a different kind, one that measures decisions against the long arc of human consequence. The trials recalled in this book illustrate that divergence with clarity. What appeared legally inevitable in the moment often came to be viewed, in retrospect, as morally insufficient. The distance between judicial outcome and historical judgment is not an indictment of judging itself, but a reminder of its limits.

Conscience enters this space not as a rival to law, but as its unfinished companion. In many of these trials, conscience was present, though not always audible in the language of the court. It spoke through acts of refusal, through arguments that stretched the boundaries of existing doctrine, and through public responses that transformed courtroom defeats into political awakenings. History records these moments not for their success in law, but for their capacity to reshape collective understanding. The authority of conscience, though denied formal recognition, survived beyond the courtroom.

The verdict of history also reveals how judicial decisions are refracted through time by the societies that inherit them. Colonial courts enforced an order they regarded as lawful and necessary, even as they failed to foresee how decisively history would later condemn that order as a system of repression. Yet legal reasoning, once released into the public domain, acquires meanings that exceed its authors. History does not erase judgments; it contextualizes them. In doing so, it exposes how law, when detached from the moral claims of its moment, may achieve finality without justice.

This awareness places a responsibility on contemporary courts. Judgment is never rendered in isolation; it enters a continuum of memory and meaning. The knowledge that today's decisions will be read by a future unbound by present anxieties should encourage deliberation that is attentive to consequence as well as correctness. Courts cannot command the verdict of history, but they can act with the humility that recognizes its eventual arrival. In that humility lies the enduring bond between law and conscience.

Why This Book Matters Now

In an age when the language of legality is invoked to justify the expansion of coercive power, this book arrives with quiet urgency. Contemporary democracies face pressures that are different in form, yet familiar in substance—the temptation to equate dissent with disruption, to treat public order as an end in itself, and to frame constitutional freedoms as conditional privileges. The trials examined here remind us that such tendencies are neither novel nor benign. They demonstrate how easily law can be made to speak the vocabulary of necessity, and how vital it is for constitutional institutions to remain alert to that drift.

The enduring relevance of this work lies in its capacity to function both as a warning and guidance. It warns against the complacency that assumes constitutional guarantees are self-executing, immune to erosion through interpretation or practice. At the same time, it offers guidance by returning us to first principles—that power must justify itself, that dissent is integral to democratic vitality, and that courts serve the Constitution best when they protect the moral agency of individuals, especially in moments of political discomfort. The past, as this book shows, does not merely explain the present; it disciplines it.

In bringing these trials together with care, balance, and intellectual honesty, Akash Vajpai has rendered a valuable service to constitutional culture. The book speaks not only to historians and lawyers, but to all who remain invested in the fragile architecture of liberty. It is hoped that this work will be read widely, reflected upon deeply, and returned to often, both as a record of what was endured and as a reminder of what must never be taken for granted.

Dr Justice D.Y. Chandrachud
25 December 2025

INTRODUCTION

At the stroke of midnight on 15 August 1947, as the world slept, India awoke to life and freedom. To rouse her from a hundred years of slumber, many endured years in prison, while others sacrificed their lives. Some faded into obscurity; others rose to glory. While some remained freedom fighters, others became founding fathers.

15 August 1947 earned its rightful place in history, yet certain other dates remain overshadowed. Freedom arrived at midnight, but before that, India witnessed the secretive late-evening execution of Bhagat Singh on 23 March 1931, and even before that, India saw a midnight court hearing on 22 July 1906, where Bal Gangadhar Tilak was sentenced to six years of imprisonment in Burma for writing articles.

We've read about many freedom fighters and their struggles in history books, but little has been written about their legal battles against the mighty British Empire. From the very beginning, the British judicial system in India was regressive and biased against Indians. The outcomes of many of these trials played a role in shaping criminal justice reforms in independent India. Most trials were held under charges of conspiracy and sedition and though the accused were convicted on one ground or another, these trials exposed the inherent injustice of the colonial legal system. Our freedom fighters often lost these legal battles and sometimes even their lives in the prime of their youth. Yet, through their fearless actions, they inspired millions, ultimately leading India to freedom.

These trials also reveal how the British manipulated the law to serve their own interests. From appointing biased Magistrates like Syed Ainuddin in the trial of Ram Prasad Bismil, to amending legal provisions during the pendency of Bhagat Singh's trial in order to deny him the right to appeal in the High Court, the British administration repeatedly bent the legal system to achieve their objectives. Many of the original proclamations, writings and revolutionary documents that emerged from these moments of confrontation with colonial authority are reproduced in the Appendices to provide direct access to the voices and ideas that shaped these trials.

This book contains 12 chapters, each recounting a different trial story rarely taught in law schools or discussed in academic circles. It begins with the INA Trial which became the final nail in the coffin of British rule in India and concludes with the story of the trial of Mangal Pandey, which ignited the fire of the 1857 rebellion or India's first freedom struggle. Coincidentally, both the first and last trial featured soldiers who had once served in the British Armed Forces.

Trial records are often tedious and filled with complex legal jargon. In this book, I have attempted to simplify them while offering historical context so that these narratives go beyond being just legal documentation. These trials also reveal lesser-known aspects of our freedom fighters that often elude traditional historical accounts. Though almost all the trials ended in convictions, resulting in executions or long imprisonments, they ultimately contributed to the freedom we now cherish. Though lost to time, these trials deserve to be remembered. Through this book, as a lawyer and student of law, I strive to bring them back into the light again.

ONE

INA TRIAL (RED FORT TRIAL)

For nearly 30 years, Jawaharlal Nehru had not donned his black robe and white band. Though trained as a lawyer in England, his association with Mahatma Gandhi had drawn him completely into the freedom movement, and he had dedicated his life to India's struggle for independence. When he was released in 1945, after spending almost three years in jail, World War II was nearing its end, and the political situation in the Indian subcontinent had changed. The British government in India decided to hold a court-martial proceeding against three senior officers of the Indian National Army (INA) who, despite being officers of the British Indian Army, had fought under Subhas Chandra Bose against the British.

These three men were Captain P.K. Sahgal (Baluch Regiment), Lieutenant Gurbaksh Singh Dhillon and Captain Shah Nawaz Khan (Punjab Regiment). They had played prominent roles in the INA's fight against the British. Although Nehru had initially disagreed with Subhas Chandra Bose and his policy of pursuing India's freedom through armed struggle, considering it contrary to Gandhi's principle of non-violence, he later took a different stand. As one of the foremost leaders of the Congress after Gandhi and Patel, Nehru was determined not to let the party repeat the mistake it had made during Bhagat Singh's trial. At that time, while Bhagat Singh and his comrades enjoyed immense public support, the Congress had kept its distance from the trial and refrained from extending legal assistance. Learning from that mistake, Nehru now resolved to personally defend the accused in the INA trial. Responding to the massive wave of public sentiment in support of the INA officers, the Congress set up a Defence Committee of eminent lawyers, with Nehru as one of its members, to defend the accused in the trial.

Venue of the Trial

In an effort to set an example, the British decided to hold court-martial proceedings against three INA officers in the Red Fort. Traditionally the seat of Mughal power, the Red Fort had also been the site where, nearly ninety years earlier, the last Mughal emperor, Bahadur Shah Zafar, was put on trial by the British for his role in the Revolt of 1857. Zafar's trial had been staged to reinforce British supremacy and to caution Indians against rebellion.

In 1945, through the INA trial, the British sought to deliver the same message: Any act of treason would be met with the severest punishment. Yet, by choosing the Red Fort, they placed the entire proceedings under intense public scrutiny. Instead of evoking fear, the trial of the three officers sparked widespread anger and fuelled a powerful wave of nationalism across the country. The British government's attempt to convict and execute these INA officers on charges of treason ultimately backfired. From Kashmir to Kanyakumari, protests erupted in every district. When British troops opened fire on demonstrators, killing several, the outrage only grew stronger.

People began observing 'INA Day' as a mark of resistance. The trial also became a powerful symbol of Hindu-Muslim-

Sikh unity. The fact that the accused—a Hindu, a Muslim, and a Sikh—represented India's three major communities deeply moved every section of society. Not just the Congress, but the Muslim League and the Akali Dal also appealed jointly to the Viceroy for their release, declaring the accused to be patriots who had fought for India's freedom. Yet, the British went ahead with the trial. This proved to be a grave miscalculation. This trial had stirred the emotions of the Indian public in a way which had never been seen before. Bhulabhai J. Desai, the leading defence counsel, even warned openly that if the government attempted to execute any of the accused, an armed uprising in India could not be ruled out.

History of INA

During World War II, when Singapore fell to the Japanese in February 1942, nearly 40,000 Indian soldiers fighting for the British surrendered to Japan and were taken as prisoners of war. On 16 February 1942, Colonel Hunt, representing the British Army, officially handed these Indian soldiers over to Major Fujiwara of the Imperial Japanese Army at Farrer Park, Singapore. Major Fujiwara then transferred them to Captain Mohan Singh, who informed the prisoners that, with Japanese support, the INA had been formed to secure India's independence. Both the Japanese authorities and Captain Mohan Singh sought to enlist these men in the struggle for India's liberation. Importantly, while Indian soldiers were handed over, British prisoners of war were segregated and not transferred.

This act left the Indian soldiers feeling betrayed and abandoned, as the British had so readily surrendered them to the Japanese. The incident also made them realize that if Britain could so easily give up one of its strongest naval bases like Singapore, it would eventually abandon India too, leaving it vulnerable. This sense of betrayal deeply motivated many to join the INA and fight for their country's freedom. At Farrer Park, the overwhelming majority of Indian soldiers expressed their willingness to enlist in the INA. Thus, with the support of the Japanese government and under the leadership of Captain Mohan Singh, guided by Rash Bihari Bose, the INA formally came into being.

But soon, differences emerged between Captain Mohan Singh and the Japanese authorities, ultimately leading to the arrest of Mohan Singh. In 1943, the INA was reconstituted, and after the arrival of Subhas Chandra Bose in Singapore, he took over its leadership. Under Bose, the INA was infused with fresh energy and determination. He also established the Provisional Government of Free India, known as Azad Hind, with the INA as its army. Soon after its formation, this provisional government under Bose declared war on Britain and the United States, set up a cabinet and founded the Azad Hind Bank, which raised nearly 20 crore rupees from the 2.5 million Indians living in Southeast Asia. To regulate the functioning of the army, the Indian National Army Act was enacted. The Indian Independence League, initially headed by Rash Bihari Bose, too later came under the leadership of Subhas Chandra Bose, who assumed charge as the supreme commander of both the League and the INA. Under him, the INA had two main objectives: to fight the British along India's northeast frontier and secure independence, and to safeguard the interests of Indians living in Southeast Asia.

The Azad Hind government operated from Singapore, and the Japanese even put territories such as the Andaman and Nicobar Islands and parts of present-day Manipur under its control. INA soldiers fought bravely against the British and captured areas like Moirang where they hoisted the national flag for the first time. However, with Japan's surrender, the INA was left without support or supplies, forcing many soldiers to either fall in battle or surrender. Those who survived were taken prisoners, and the British decided to court-martial three INA officers among them.

Initially, the Indian public remained unaware of the INA's activities due to strict wartime censorship imposed during World War II by the British government. But with Japan's surrender and the end of the war, censorship was lifted, and reports of the INA's bravery and Bose's leadership began reaching the masses through Indian newspapers. Indians were electrified to learn that Bose had not only raised a fully Indian army but also defeated the British on several fronts in the Northeast. Japan's surrender, however, shattered Bose's grand vision of liberating India. The INA had rallied under the war cry of 'Chalo Dilli', aiming to unfurl the Indian flag at the Red Fort, the symbol of former Mughal power. Ironically, even though they were not able to march into Delhi as victorious soldiers, the INA officers did enter the Red Fort, this time as prisoners on trial. Paradoxically, it was not their battles on the battlefield but their presence in Delhi as accused that truly stirred the imagination of the Indian people.

THE TRIAL

The court-martial proceedings commenced on 5 November 1945 and continued until 31 December 1945.

Judges

1. Major-General Alan Bruce Blaxland
2. Brigadier A.G.H. Bourke
3. Lt Col. C.R. Stott
4. Lt Col. T.I. Stevenson
5. Lt Col. Nasir Ali Khan
6. Major B. Pritam Singh
7. Major Banwari Lal

Prosecution's Advocates

The seriousness with which the British Government viewed this case is evident from its decision to appoint Sir Naushirwan P. Engineer, the then Advocate General of India and the highest law officer of the time, to lead the prosecution in the Trial.

Defence's Advocates

The following lawyers appeared on behalf of the accused as members of the Defence Committee constituted by the Congress:

1. Pandit Jawaharlal Nehru
2. Sir Tej Bahadur Sapru
3. Bhulabhai J. Desai
4. Dr Kailash Nath Katju
5. R.B. Badri Das
6. Mr Asaf Ali
7. Sir Dalip Singh, Former Judge, Lahore High Court
8. Sir Tek Chand, Former Judge, Lahore High Court
9. Mr P.N. Sen, Former Judge, Patna High Court
10. Mr Inder Deo Dua
11. Mr Rajendra Narain

12. Mr Sri Narain Andley
13. Mr Gobind Saran Singh
14. Mr Jugal Kishore Khanna
15. Mr Mayank Lal Vakil
16. Mr Sultan Yar Khan
17. Shiv Kumar Shastri

When Sir Tej Bahadur Sapru fell ill, it was Bhulabhai J. Desai who took charge of leading the defence team. A distinguished lawyer of his era and a staunch Congressman, Desai had earlier made earnest efforts to bring the Desai-Liaquat Pact to fruition at a time when most Congress leaders were imprisoned and tried his best to stop the partition of the country. But his efforts failed when both Muslim League and the Congress refused to recognize this pact.

Despite his advanced age, Bhulabhai did not hesitate to shoulder the responsibility of defending the accused in one of the most sensational trials of the time. The court-martial was conducted on the second floor of a building that had served as the dormitory since its construction in 1868 inside the Red Fort. Since Desai found it difficult to climb the stairs, his supporters carried him up in a chair so that he could be present and argue the case. Bhulabhai's role as leading counsel in this high-pressure trial marked his final great act of service for the Congress and the nation. The immense strain of the proceedings took a heavy toll on his health, allowing him only a few more months of life. He passed away in May 1946, barely four months after the conclusion of the trial.

Charges

The three INA officers were charged with waging war against the King (Section 121 of IPC) through various acts carried out jointly at different locations during the INA campaign outside India. They were also accused of murdering certain individuals whom they had executed or punished in the course of their duties as INA officers, along with charges of abetment to murder. These murder and abetment charges specifically related to the shooting of INA members for desertion and for attempting to communicate with the enemy (British).

Prosecution's Arguments

The prosecution, relying upon the testimony of several witnesses, argued that the accused officers had recruited men for the INA, participated in its organization, issued directions and orders to fight against His Majesty's forces (British Army), and themselves taken part in combat. They argued that soon after the fall of Singapore, the accused not only joined the INA but also attempted, through lectures, to persuade other prisoners of war to renounce their allegiance to the Crown. The prosecution further asserted that the very act of declaring a so-called Provisional Government of Free India was in itself an offence, and no such declaration could provide immunity.

The purpose for which the war was waged, they argued, was irrelevant; the act remained an offence regardless of the motive. The prosecution emphasized that the present court, convened as a court-martial, was constituted under the Indian Army Act, and was not an international tribunal where international legal points could be raised. The court's mandate was to try individuals in accordance with the Indian Army Act for offences punishable under that Act and under the Indian Penal Code. Prosecution submitted that the word 'law' in Section 79 of the IPC referred only to the law in force in British India and not international law. Recognition of the court's legitimacy by foreign states, they maintained, had no bearing on the rights of the Crown over its own subjects. It was further argued by the prosecution that the so-called Provisional Government of Free India never truly existed as a government: it neither occupied any territory nor collected a single piece of revenue or tax. Its existence, prosecution argued, depended entirely on Japan's conquest of India, after which power would supposedly be handed over to the Indians. In reality, it was a government only on paper. Although Japan had requested its allies to recognize this government, and they had done so, Japan itself never ceded the Andaman and Nicobar Islands or any other territory for it to administer.

The prosecution argued that the accused were not merely civilians but commissioned officers in the Indian Army. By waging war against His Majesty, the King, they had, by implication, deserted the army in which they held commissions. According to prosecution, Section 41 of the Indian Army Act made clear that any person subject to the Act who committed a civil offence, whether in India or abroad, was guilty of an offence under military law and could be tried and punished by court-martial.

The prosecution also charged Captain Shah Nawaz with abetment of the murder of Sepoy Mohammed Husain near Popa Hill, Burma, on 29 March 1945. According to the testimony of witnesses, Captain Shah Nawaz had informed Mohammed Husain that he was sentenced to death for attempting to desert INA and for persuading others to follow. The execution of Mohammed Husain was, thus, carried out under his command and order.

Similarly, Lieutenant Dhillon was charged with the murder of four sepoys (Hari Singh, Dulli Chand, Daryao Singh and

Dharam Singh), while Captain Sahgal was accused of abetting those killings. Referring to Sections 107 and 109 of the Indian Penal Code, the prosecution emphasized that instigation or aiding an act constituted abetment, and liability remained even if the accused was not physically present at the scene. Thus, both Captain Sahgal and Captain Shah Nawaz were charged with abetment rather than direct involvement in the killings.

The prosecution presented thirty witnesses, who deposed about the formation and growth of the INA and the provisional government, the operational functions of various INA units, and the specific roles played by each of the accused in these activities.

In conclusion, Advocate General Naushirwan Engineer, presenting the prosecution's case, maintained that the evidence proved the accused guilty of desertion, waging war against the King, and abetment of murder. He wrapped up his arguments in the following words:[1]

> In conclusion, I submit that all the charges against all the accused have been proved beyond any reasonable doubt. There is no defence in law to the charges against the accused. There is a good deal of evidence to the effect that what the accused did was done by them not with any mercenary motive, but out of what the accused bona fide consider to be patriotic motives and impelled by a sense, whether wise or misguided, of doing service to India. This, while not affording any defence to the accused in law, may legitimately be taken into consideration on the question of punishment, if the court's findings on the charges are against the accused.

---

[1]Ram, Moti, *The Historic Trials in the Red Fort*, Nandy Enterprises, Noida, 2021.

> So far as the court is concerned, its hands are tied in the matter of punishment. The minimum punishment which this court can give is transportation for life. If the court's finding is against the accused, but the court feels on the evidence before it that the case is a fit one for mitigation of punishment, it is open to the court to add a rider to its finding and sentence to that effect for the consideration of the confirming officer.

Defence's Arguments

Bhulabhai Desai, who was leading the defence team, advanced a very unique line of arguments, raising issues involving military law, constitutional law, international law and politics. He argued that the accused were the members of an organized army (INA) engaged in waging war against the King and that their actions could not be regarded as personal crimes. Relying upon established principles of international law, he maintained that the accused were entitled to raise arms for the liberation of their country as part of an organized force operating under the authority of a provisional government.

Consequently, the acts committed by them in their capacity as members of such a force could not constitute offences under the municipal law of India like IPC. It was argued that the accused enjoyed immunity under international law for the offences they were charged with under the Indian Penal Code. He argued:[2]

> [...] It is not all a case of what you might call three individuals waging war against the King. The evidence

[2]Ibid.

> amply bears out the fact that these men charged before you were a part of an organized army which waged war against the king even according to the prosecution. Therefore, the case before the court is not a personal case of any kind or sort. The honour and the law of the Indian National Army are on Trial before this Court. What is now on trial before the court is the right to wage war with immunity on the part of a subject race for their liberation. A nation or part of nation does reach a stage where it is entitled to wage war for its liberation.

Mr Desai further contended that the INA functioned under the authority of a provisional government (Azad Hind) which had been formally established and proclaimed following the overthrow of British rule and their allies in Southeast Asia. This provisional government, he argued, was constituted with the consent of nearly 2.5 million Indians residing in those territories. Its mandate was to administer the affairs of the nation until a permanent national government of Azad Hind could be established on Indian soil. According to him, the provisional government, under the leadership of Subhas Chandra Bose, was a duly organized authority. The Indian Independence League acted as its executive, and the Government itself had been recognized by several Axis powers, including Germany, Japan, Italy, etc. Such recognition, he asserted, not only validated its existence but also conferred upon it the right to declare war for the objective it pursued.

Consequently, once a State is recognized as competent to declare war, its military operations are governed by the international laws of war. The provisional government, according to him, was properly constituted, possessed its own insignia, emblems and officers appointed in regular form, and it enacted the Indian National Army Act to regulate its forces. The INA itself was created with two principal objectives: the foremost being the liberation of India, and the secondary, though significant, being the protection of Indian inhabitants in Burma, Malaya and Singapore.

The Japanese government, Mr Desai argued, had ceded the Andaman and Nicobar Islands to the provisional government of Azad Hind, which renamed them Swaraj and Shaheed, thereby incorporating them into the liberated territory. In addition, this provisional government exercised administrative authority over certain areas in Northeast India that had previously been under British control. On this basis, he argued that the newly constituted Indian State was in a position to declare war, and once such a declaration was made, any acts committed in the prosecution of that war fell outside the scope of municipal law. To illustrate, he advanced a hypothetical case: if during the course of war a German soldier were to shoot two, three, or even ten British nationals in England and were subsequently captured there, the issue of whether he could be charged with murder would arise. His submission was that during the prosecution of war the ordinary municipal law of that country was inapplicable. Invoking principles of international law, Desai contended that when two independent nations, or States, engaged in war against each other, the acts committed by their soldiers in the lawful prosecution of such war, except those amounting to war crimes, fell beyond the scope of municipal law. He further submitted that this Provisional Government of Free India had the legitimate right to wage war, and it did so with the objective of liberating the nation.

Mr Desai also argued that even if the acts in question were examined under Section 79 of the Indian Penal Code, Section 79 of the Code provided for a general defence for acts committed under the belief that they were justified by 'law'. He argued that no offence was made out where a person acted under belief. Mr Desai further argued that the expression 'law' in Section 79 must be interpreted to include not merely municipal law but also the principles of international law. In his unique style of arguing and unconventional illustration, Bhulabhai compared the INA men with George Washington and his followers of 1776, who had rightly repudiated their earlier allegiance to the British Crown in pursuit of their country's independence. The key legal question before the court according to Mr Desai was whether the accused were traitors under the Indian Army Act or lawful soldiers under the INA Act.

He further maintained that any alleged atrocities on INA soldiers by the accused were punishments under the INA Act. The defence under Bhulabhai examined twelve witnesses, including S.A. Ayer (Propaganda Minister of the Azad Hind Government), Lt Col. Logananda (Chief Commissioner of the Andaman Islands appointed by the Azad Hind government) and several Japanese officials, whose evidence sought to prove that the INA and the provisional government were independent entities, free from Japanese control, and entitled under international law to recognition as a legitimate army and State. Bhulabhai's ex tempore arguments continued for two full days, whereas Sir Naushirwan Engineer, representing the prosecution, concluded his submissions in about four hours.

Concluding his submissions before the court, Bhulabhai remarked:[3]

> If you find that there is a de facto political organisation sufficient in numbers, sufficient in character and sufficient in resources to constitute itself capable of declaring and making war with an organized army, your verdict must be in favour of these men-no more and no less than the verdict on your own men for killing others, of which act you are justly proud.

Judgment Day

After hearing the closing arguments from all sides on 31 December 1945, the President of the Court, Major-General Alan Bruce Blaxland, announced the termination of the open court proceedings. The court then adjourned to deliberate on the sentencing. On 3 January 1946, through a communique published in *The Gazette of India*, the court found all three accused, Captain Shah Nawaz Khan, Captain P.K. Sahgal, and Lieutenant Gurbaksh Singh Dhillon, guilty of waging war against the King-Emperor.

Additionally, Captain Shah Nawaz Khan was also convicted of abetment to murder, while Lt Dhillon was acquitted of the charge of murder and Captain Sahgal was acquitted of the charge of abetment to murder. Now when it came to passing a judgment to all three accused on the charge of waging the war against the King, the court observed:[4]

---

[3]Setalvad, M.C., *Bhulabhai Desai*, Publications Division (Ministry of Information and Broadcasting, Government of India), New Delhi, 1981.

[4]Ram, Moti, *The Historic Trials in the Red Fort*, Nandy Enterprises, Noida, 2021.

> [...] Having found the accused guilty of the charge of waging war, the court was bound to sentence the accused either to death or to transportation for life: no lesser sentence was permissible under the law. The sentence of the court on all three accused is transportation for life, cashiering and forfeiture of arrears of pay and allowances.

Amidst the charged political atmosphere, the British recognized that imposing severe punishments on the accused could provoke a rebellion or mutiny akin to that of 1857, while granting them an outright acquittal would weaken the government's authority and prestige. In his report to the Viceroy, General Claude Auchinleck, the Commander-in-Chief of India, cautioned that upholding the sentences of transportation would only turn the officers into martyrs and further intensify the campaign of bitterness and racial antagonism against the British.

Following this, the Viceroy and Auchinleck held urgent consultations and concluded that the punishments required reconsideration in light of the overwhelming wave of public sympathy for the INA. As a middle path, although the court pronounced all three officers guilty and sentenced them to life imprisonment, the verdict was placed before the Commander-in-Chief for confirmation. Since no sentence of a court-martial attained validity without approval from the confirming authority, the case was placed before General Auchinleck. Taking into account the powerful surge of public sentiment, he decided to remit the sentences and ordered the immediate release of all the accused, while retaining the lesser penalties of cashiering and forfeiture of pay arrears and allowances. In an official communiqué issued on 3 January 1946, the court observed:[5]

---

[5]Ibid.

> The Commander-in-Chief has decided, therefore, to treat all three accused in the same way in the matter of sentence, and to remit the sentences of transportation for life against all three accused. He has, however, confirmed the sentence of cashiering and forfeiture of arrears of pay and allowances, since it is in all circumstances a most serious crime for an officer or soldier to throw off his allegiance and wage war against the State. This is a principle which it is essential to uphold in the interests of the stability of any governments by law established, present or future.

In the end, it was the will of the Indian people that prevailed. On 3 January 1946 itself, all three officers were released from their confinement at the Red Fort, where they had spent the previous three months as prisoners. The news spread through the city like wildfire, prompting crowds to gather at the Red Fort to welcome their heroes. After their release, the trio proceeded directly to the home of Asaf Ali, a leading counsel of their defence team. Along the way, they were met by an overwhelming wave of supporters, who garlanded them, lifted them onto their shoulders, and rent the sky with cries of 'Jai Hind', 'Inqilab Zindabad', and 'Subhas Babu Amar Rahe'. At that time, Nehru, speaking at a public meeting in Karachi, paid his tribute to the spirit of Subhas Chandra Bose and the patriotism of the INA, remarking: 'The true triumph belonged to the Indian people who had already rendered their judgment, and their verdict was far too powerful to be ignored.'

Aftermath

The INA trial was arguably the most significant trial in the history of British India. It not only inspired the Indian freedom movement but also accelerated the final phase of India's struggle for independence from British rule. The trial sparked an unprecedented wave of nationalist sentiment that directly challenged the legitimacy of British authority and compelled the British Commander-in-Chief to remit the life imprisonment sentences handed down to the accused by the court. The INA trial ignited a fire that swiftly spread through the British Indian armed forces.

Within a few days from the date of acquittal of the accused in the INA Trials in February 1946, over a thousand Indian Navy personnel revolted against British rule. This shook the foundation of the British Empire in India. The British officers received inputs from their intelligence department that the loyalty of native soldiers was eroding and they could no longer depend on the Indian armed forces to rule in India. Exhausted by World War II, Britain no longer had the strength to control a vast country like India, especially when the loyalty of its native soldiers, the backbone of its empire, was crumbling. With memories of 1857 still haunting them, the British feared another mutiny and quickly dispatched the Cabinet Mission with the aim of granting India full independence. The INA trial inspired widespread resistance within the British Indian armed forces and can rightly be described as the final nail in the coffin of the British Empire in India. Just as the trial of Bahadur Shah Zafar had marked the end of one chapter of Indian history, the INA trials symbolized the closing of another chapter, the decline and final collapse of British rule in India.

The conclusion of this chapter would be incomplete without recalling Jawaharlal Nehru's letter dated 4 May 1946, to General Claude Auchinleck. In this letter, while expressing his gratitude to Auchinleck for his decision to remit the life transportation sentence of the three INA officers, Nehru also explained why the INA Trial became a powerful symbol of the Indian struggle for independence. An extract from that letter is reproduced here:[6]

> Though I had sensed the mood of the Indian people, I had not fully realized how far it went in this direction. Within a few weeks the story of the I.N.A. had percolated to the remotest villages in India and everywhere there was admiration for them and apprehension as to their possible fate. No political organization, however strong and efficient, could have produced this enormous reaction in India. It was one of those rare things which just fit into the mood of the people, reflect as it were, and provide an opportunity for the public to give expression to that mood. The reason for this was obvious. Individuals were not known nor were many facts known to the public. The story as it developed seemed to the people just another aspect of India's struggle for independence and the individuals concerned became symbols in the public mind. Whether one agrees with this or not, one should at least understand how things happen and what forces lie behind them. The widespread popular enthusiasm was surprising enough, but even more surprising was a similar reaction of a very large number of regular Indian Army officers and men. Something had touched them deeply. This kind of thing is not done and cannot be done by politicians or agitators or the like. It is this fundamental aspect of the I.N.A. question that has to be

---

[6]Setalvad, M.C., *Bhulabhai Desai*, Publications Division (Ministry of Information and Broadcasting, Government of India), New Delhi, 1981.

> borne in mind. All other aspects. however, important, are secondary.

It would not be wrong to say that despite the brilliant arguments of Mr Desai it was the collective will of the Indian people that saved not only the lives of the INA officers but also safeguarded the honour and prestige of the nation. In such circumstances, any claim that the British could continue to rule India by force lost its credibility. After independence, the lives of the three officers took different paths. Captain Shah Nawaz Khan, though his family migrated to Pakistan during Partition, chose to remain in India. He went on to serve as a Member of Parliament from Meerut four times and held ministerial positions in the Government of India, enjoying a successful political career. Captain P.K. Sahgal married Captain Lakshmi Swaminathan in March 1947, the head of the INA's women's wing. Lieutenant Gurbaksh Singh Dhillon lived a long and respected life, receiving the Padma Bhushan in 1998 in recognition of his service to the nation.

TWO

TRIAL OF MAHATMA GANDHI

On 11 March 1922, during a courtroom proceeding before Additional District Magistrate Mr L.N. Brown, the accused, clad only in simple dhoti with nothing above his waist, was asked to state his name, age, caste and occupation. With quiet dignity, he responded, 'Name: Mahatma Gandhi, age: 53, caste: Hindu-Bania, occupation: farmer and weaver.'

The magistrate initially frowned, visibly taken aback. Standing before him was not a mere commoner, but the very man who had recently shaken the foundations of British rule with a sweeping nationwide non-cooperation movement. And yet, Gandhi chose to introduce himself with utmost humility and simplicity.

Gandhi, in his trial, stood accused of sedition under the notorious Section 124A[7] of the Indian Penal Code, a provision frequently used by the British to silence nationalist voices. The same provision had earlier been invoked to exile Bal Gangadhar Tilak to Burma for his writings against colonial rule. After World War I, Gandhi and many Indians had hoped that the British would reward Indian loyalty with dominion status and other political reforms for supporting

[7]Section 124A of the Indian Penal Code (IPC) deals with the offence of sedition.

them in the war. Instead, the British introduced the draconian Rowlatt Act,[8] which permitted arrests without warrant and curtailed civil liberties.

The Jallianwala Bagh massacre in Amritsar during the festival of Baisakhi shattered whatever illusions Gandhi still held about British intentions. In response, Gandhi launched his first nationwide Non-Cooperation Movement in 1920. Students walked out of government schools and colleges, foreign goods and clothes were boycotted, taxes went unpaid, and jails overflowed with peaceful protestors. Though largely non-violent, the movement saw sporadic instances of unrest and violence. One such tragic episode occurred on 4 February 1922 in Chauri-Chaura, near Gorakhpur, where enraged protestors torched a police station, killing 22 policemen. Deeply disturbed by this act of violence, Gandhi called off the movement, unwilling to compromise on his core principle of ahimsa (non-violence). His sudden withdrawal sent shockwaves across the country. Thousands who had sacrificed and endured suffering felt disillusioned and betrayed.

The British, on the other hand, breathed a sigh of relief. The Viceroy, sensing an opportunity, moved swiftly. On 10 March 1922, Gandhi was arrested from Sabarmati Ashram in Ahmedabad. When he was produced in court, the atmosphere was electric. The premises were packed with supporters, and a platoon of the British Indian Army stood on standby. Prominent Congress leaders, including Madan Mohan Malviya, Sarojini Naidu, Pandit Jawaharlal Nehru, Sardar Vallabhbhai Patel and others, were in court. Capturing the charged atmosphere in the

---

[8]Rowlatt Act was named after a British judge, Sidney Rowlatt, who chaired the committee responsible for drafting this controversial law.

courtroom, Sarojini Naidu described this moment of history into the following words: [9]

> A convict and a criminal in the eyes of the law. Nevertheless [sic], the entire court rose in an act of spontaneous homage when Mahatma Gandhi entered a frail, serene, indomitable figure in a coarse and scanty loin cloth.

Mahatma Gandhi was charged with inciting disaffection against the British government through four articles published in *Young India* magazine. The articles in question were titled: 'Disaffection a Virtue' (15 June 1921), 'Tampering with Loyalty' (29 September 1921), 'The Puzzle and Its Solution' (15 December 1921), and 'Shaking the Manes' (23 February 1922).[10] In support of its case, the prosecution examined five witnesses before the court. However, both Mahatma Gandhi and his co-accused, Shankar Lal, the printer and publisher of *Young India*, chose not to cross-examine any of them.

The trial of Mahatma Gandhi attracted widespread attention from both national and international media. Many drew parallels between Gandhi's trial and the historic trial of Socrates in the 4th century BC where Socrates was accused of corrupting the youth of Athens. Reflecting on this comparison, Justice J.M. Shelat, former Judge of the Supreme Court of India, remarked that:[11]

> Barring the trial of Socrates, there is perhaps no trial in the history of mankind comparable to that of Gandhiji,

---

[9]Anand, Mulk Raj, *The Historic Trial of Mahatma Gandhi*, National Council of Educational Research and Training, New Delhi, 1987.

[10]Please see *Appendix 2* for reference.

[11]Ibid.

> which stimulated so much interest and whose influence in the life of humanity has been so profound, involving, as it did, the issue of morality versus law. The similarity of attitude adopted by Socrates and Gandhiji towards the tribunals which tried them, is at once manifest. For each placed truth above the law and sought the punishment which the branch of law warranted.

THE TRIAL

Emperor v. Mohandas Karamchand Gandhi & Anr.
Divisional Commissioner at Shahi Bagh, Ahmedabad
11 March 1922

After the prosecution concluded its evidence, Magistrate Mr L.N. Brown turned to Mahatma Gandhi and asked him whether he wished to say anything in his defence against the evidence presented by the prosecution. Gandhi responded calmly, stating that he would present his case at the appropriate time, and added that he intended to plead guilty to the charge of inciting disaffection against the government. He also acknowledged that he was the editor of *Young India* and that the alleged articles read in court were indeed authored by him. Mr Brown formally recorded Gandhi's statement, noting that Gandhi had not wished to summon any witnesses in his defence and had no objection to the case being committed[12] to the Sessions Court without delay. While forwarding the

---

[12]Committed to the Sessions Court means that a Magistrate has transferred a criminal case to the Sessions Court for trial, because the offence involved is serious and falls outside the jurisdiction of a Magistrate to try.

matter to the Sessions Court, Magistrate L.N. Brown issued the following order:

> The accused having been charged with promoting sedition by certain articles published in Young India, of which accused number one is the Editor and accused No. 2 the Printer. They have stated that it is their intention to plead guilty to the charge at the proper time. I, L.N. Brown, Additional District Magistrate, hereby charge you, Mohandas Karamchand Gandhi as follows:
>
> 'That you being the Editor of the Paper "Young India" on or about the 29th day of September, 1921, the 15th day of December, 1921, and the 23rd day of February 1922, at Ahmedabad, did write the words contained in the appendix to this charge, and by these written words did bring, or did attempt to bring, into hatred or contempt, or did excite, or did attempt to excite disaffection towards His Majesty, or the Government established by law in British India, and thereby committed offences punishable under Section 124A of the Indian Penal Code and within the cognisance of the Court of Sessions.
>
> And I hereby direct that you be tried by the said court on the said charge. I have, therefore, no alternative, but to commit you to the Court of Sessions for offences appearing too serious for me to dispose of the case myself'.

Sessions Court's Proceedings

18 March 1922

When Mahatma Gandhi's case reached the Sessions Court, it was presided over by C.N. Broomfield, the District and

Sessions Judge of Ahmedabad. The trial commenced on 18 March 1922. The central issue in this historic trial was of great moral and political significance: Was Gandhi justified in presenting political rebellion as a moral duty?

The courtroom was packed with prominent visitors from Ahmedabad and from across the country. Among them were members of the Working Committee of the Indian National Congress and delegates from the Provincial Congress Committee. The prosecution, representing the British government, was led by the Advocate General, Sir J.T. Strangman. When Mahatma Gandhi arrived, the courtroom was already overflowing. Judge Broomfield took his seat at 12 p.m. and directed the court clerk to read out the charges. The clerk formally informed Gandhi that he was being tried under Section 124A of the Indian Penal Code (Sedition). After the charges were read and explained, the Judge asked both Mahatma Gandhi and his co-accused, Shankar Lal Banker, whether they would plead guilty or face trial. Both men pleaded guilty. Despite their plea accepting guilt, the Advocate General requested that the case proceed to trial. Judge Broomfield declined this request and instead moved directly to pronounce the sentence.

However, before doing so, he offered Gandhi an opportunity to speak. Gandhi accepted the court's decision with a calm smile and sought permission to read a statement in his defence. The Judge requested a copy for the official record, but Gandhi insisted on reading it aloud first and submitting it later. The atmosphere in the courtroom became electric. It is hard to capture in words the weight of that moment. Gandhi spoke for fifteen minutes, and every individual present, be it the Judge, the Advocate General or the political leaders of Congress, listened in complete attention. No one wanted to miss a single word of what would become a historic and unforgettable courtroom address. For the readers' convenience, we now present the complete statement delivered by Mahatma Gandhi during this historic trial.

Statement of Mahatma Gandhi[13]

> I owe it perhaps to the Indian public and to public in England to placate which this prosecution is mainly taken up: that I should explain why, from a staunch loyalist and cooperator, I have become an uncompromising disaffectionist and non-cooperator. To the Court too I should say why I plead guilty to the charge of promoting disaffection towards the Government established by law in India. My public life began in 1893 in South Africa in troubled weather. My first contact with British authority in that country was not of a happy character. I discovered that, as a man and an Indian, I had no rights. More correctly, I discovered that I had no rights as a man because I was an Indian.
>
> But I was not baffled, I thought that this treatment of Indians was an excrescence upon a system that was intrinsically and mainly good. I gave the Government my voluntary and hearty cooperation, criticising it freely where I felt it was faulty but never wishing its destruction.
>
> Consequently, when the existence of the Empire was threatened in 1899 by the Boer challenge, I offered my services to it, raised a volunteer ambulance corps and

[13]Anand, Mulk Raj, *The Historic Trial of Mahatma Gandhi*, National Council of Educational Research and Training, New Delhi, 1987.

served at several actions that took place for the relief of Ladysmith. Similarly, in 1906, at the time of Zulu revolt, I raised a stretcher-bearer party and served till the end of the rebellion. On both these occasions I received medals and was even mentioned in despatches. For my work in South Africa, I was given by Lord Hardinge a Kaiser-i-Hind Gold Medal. When the war broke out in 1914 between England and Germany, I raised a volunteer ambulance corps in London, consisting of the then resident Indians in London chiefly students. Its work was acknowledged by the authorities to be valuable. Lastly in India, when a special appeal was made at the war conference in Delhi in 1918 by Lord Chelmsford for recruits, I struggled, at the cost of my health, to raise a corps in Kheda and the response was being made when the hostilities ceased and the orders were received that no more recruits were wanted. In all these efforts at service I was actuated by the belief that it was possible by such services to gain a status of full equality in the Empire for my countrymen.

The first shock came in the shape of the Rowlatt Act, a law designed to rob the people of all real freedom. I felt called upon to lead an intensive agitation against it. Then followed the Punjab horrors beginning with the massacre of Jallianwala Bagh and culminating in crawling orders, public floggings and other indescribable humiliations. I discovered too that the plighted word of the Prime Minister to the Mussalmans of India regarding the integrity of Turkey and the Holy Places of Islam was not likely to be fulfilled. But, in spite of the forebodings and the grave warnings of friends, at the Amritsar Congress in

1919, I fought for cooperation and working the Montagu-Chelmsford reforms, hoping that the Prime Minister would redeem his promise to the Indian Mussalmans, that the Punjab wound would be healed and that the reforms, inadequate and unsatisfactory though they were, marked a new era of hope in the life of India.

But all that hope was shattered. The Khilafat promise was not to be redeemed. The Punjab crime was whitewashed and most culprits went not only unpublished but remained in service and some continued to draw pensions from the Indian revenue, and in some cases were even rewarded. I saw to that not only did the reforms not mark a change of heart, but they were only a method of further draining India of her wealth and of prolonging her servitude.

I came reluctantly to the conclusion that the British connection had made India more helpless than she ever was before politically and economically. A disarmed India has no power of resistance against any aggressor if she wanted to engage in an armed conflict with him. So much is this the case that some of our best men consider that India must take generations before she can achieve the Dominion Status. She has been so poor that she has little power of resisting famines. Before the British advent, India spun and wove, in her millions of cottages, just the supplement she needed for adding to her meagre agricultural resources. The cottage industry, so vital for India's existence, has been ruined by incredibly heartless and inhuman processes as described by English witnesses. Little do town-dwellers know how the semi-starved masses of India are slowly sinking to lifelessness.

Little do they know that their miserable comfort represents the brokerage they get for the work they do for the foreign exploiter, that the profits and the brokerage are sucked from the masses. Little do they realise that the Government established by law in British India is carried on for this exploitation of the masses. No sophistry, no jugglery in figures, can explain away the evidence that the skeletons in many villages present to the naked eye. I have no doubt whatsoever that both England and the town-dwellers of India will have to answer, if there is a God above, for this crime against humanity which is perhaps unequalled in history. The law itself in this country has been used to serve the foreign exploiter. My unbiased examination of the Punjab Martial Law cases has led me to believe that at least ninety-five per cent of convictions were wholly bad. My experience of political cases in India leads me to the conclusion that in nine out of every ten the condemned men were totally Innocent. Their crime consisted of the love of their country. In ninety-nine cases out of hundred, Justice has been denied to Indians as against Europeans in the courts of India. This is not an exaggerated picture. It is the experience of almost every Indian who has had anything to do with such cases. In my opinion the administration of the law is thus prostituted, consciously or unconsciously, for the benefit of the exploiter.

The greatest misfortune is that Englishmen and their Indian associates in the administration of the country, do not know that they are engaged in crime I have attempted to describe. I am satisfied that many Englishmen and Indian officials honestly believe that they are administering one of the best systems devised in the world and that India is making steady though slow progress. They do not know that a subtle but effective system of terrorism and an organised display of force on the one hand, and the deprivation of all powers of retaliation or self-defence on the other, have emasculated the people and induced in them the habit of simulation. This awful habit has added to the ignorance and the self-deception of the administrators.

The Section 124A, under which I am happily charged, is perhaps the prince among the political sections of the Indian Penal Code designed to suppress the liberty of the citizen. Affection cannot be manufactured or regulated by law. If one has no affection for a person or system one should be free to give the fullest expression to his disaffection, so long as he does not contemplate, promote, or incite violence. But the section under which Mr. Banker and I are charged is one under which mere promotion of disaffection is a crime. I have studied some of the cases tried under it, and I know that some of the most loved of India's patriots have been convicted under it. I consider it a privilege, therefore, to be charged under that section. I have endeavoured to give, in their briefest outline, the reasons for my disaffection, I have no personal ill will against any single administrator much less can I have any disaffection towards the King's person. But I hold it to be a virtue to be disaffected towards a Government which, in its totality, has done more harm to India than any previous system. India is less manly under the British rule than she ever was before. Holding such a belief. I consider it to be a sin to have affection

> for the system. And it has been a precious privilege for me to be able to write what I have in the various articles tendered in as evidence against me.
>
> In fact, I believed that I have rendered a service to India and England by showing in non-cooperation the way out of the unnatural state in which both are living. In my humble opinion, non-cooperation has been deliberately expressed in violence to the evil-doer. I am endeavouring to show to my countrymen that violent non-cooperation only multiplies evil, and that as evil can only be sustained by violence, withdrawal of support of evil requires complete abstention from violence. Non-violence implies voluntary submission to the penalty for non-cooperation with evil. I am here, therefore, to invite and submit cheerfully to the highest penalty that can be inflicted upon me for what in law is a deliberate crime and what appears to me to be the highest duty of a citizen. The only course open to you, the Judge, is either to resign your post and thus disassociate yourself from evil, if you feel that the law you are called upon to administer is an evil and that in reality I am innocent; or to inflict on me the severest penalty if you believe that the system and the law you are assisting to administer are good for the people of this country and that my activity is therefore injurious to the public weal.

As Gandhi read his statement aloud, it was nothing short of electrifying. The clarity of his thoughts, his unwavering faith in his principles and his fearless demeanour had an immediate and profound impact on the audience. It felt like a powerful scene from a film where Gandhi was delivering each word with conviction, while the spectators sat in awe, utterly captivated. In that moment, it became difficult to tell who was truly on trial: Was it Gandhi standing before a British judge, or was it the British government standing before the Court of God and humanity? Judge C.N. Broomfield, bound by his duty, reluctantly sentenced Mahatma Gandhi to six years of imprisonment and awarded one year to his co-accused, Shankarlal Banker. However, before pronouncing the sentence on Gandhi, the Judge took a moment to express his thoughts and sentiments about him in the following words:[14]

> Mr. Gandhi, you have made my task easy in the way by pleading guilty to the charge. Nevertheless what remains, namely the determination of a just sentence, is perhaps as difficult a proposition as a judge in this country could have to face. The law is no respecter of persons. Nevertheless, it will be impossible to ignore the fact that you are in a different category from any person I have tried or am likely to have to try. It would be impossible to ignore the fact that in the eyes of millions of your countrymen, you are a great patriot and a great leader. Even those who differ from you in politics look upon you as a man of high ideals and of noble and of even saintly life. I have to deal with you in one character only. It is not my duty and I do not presume to judge or criticise you in any other character. It is my duty to judge you as a man subject to the law, who, by his own admission, has broken the law and committed what, to an ordinary man, must appear to be grave offence against the State. I do not forget that you have consistently preached against

[14]Gandhi, M.K., *The Law and The Lawyers*, S.B. Kher (ed.), Navjivan Trust, Ahmedabad, 1962.

> violence and that you have on many occasions, as I am willing to believe, done much to prevent violence. But having regard to the nature of your political teaching and the nature of many of those to whom it was addressed, how you could have continued to believe that violence would not be the inevitable consequence, it passes my capacity to understand. There are probably few people in India, who do not sincerely regret that you should have made it impossible for any Government to leave you at liberty. But it is so. I am trying to balance what is due to you against what appears to me to be necessary in the interest of the public. And I propose in passing sentence to followthe precedent of the case in many respects similar to this case that was decided some twelve years ago. I mean the case against Bal Gangadhar Tilak under the same section. The sentence that was passed upon him as finally stood was a sentence of simple imprisonment for six years. You will not consider it unreasonable, I think, that you should be classed with Mr. Tilak, i.e. a sentence of two years in simple imprisonment on each count of the charge, six years in all, which I feel it my duty to pass upon you. And I should like to say in doing so that if the course of events in India should make it possible for the Government to reduce the period and release you, no one will be better pleased than I.

After announcing the sentence, Judge C.N. Broomfield rose from his seat and surprisingly bowed respectfully to Mahatma Gandhi. It was perhaps the first time in the history of any courtroom where a judge bowed before the very man he was sentencing. No wonder the world called him Mahatma. In response, Mr Gandhi also graciously bowed back. The moment

Judge Broomfield retired to his chambers, an emotional wave swept through the courtroom; many in the audience began to cry and several Congress leaders gathered around Gandhi, overcome with emotion. Some even fell at his feet, sobbing, while cries of 'Mahatma Gandhi Ki Jai' echoed through the courtroom.

Amidst the emotion, Gandhi remained calm and composed, smiling warmly at everyone who came to greet him. Eventually, police officers stepped in to disperse the crowd and requested Gandhi to accompany them, as a police vehicle was waiting outside to take him to Sabarmati Jail. Gandhi, with characteristic humility, complied without resistance, bidding farewell to all those who had gathered in his support. And thus concluded one of the most historic trials in India's freedom struggle.

Aftermath

The trial of Mahatma Gandhi marked a historic chapter in India's freedom struggle. Gandhi neither summoned any witnesses nor presented any evidence in his defence. He willingly accepted the punishment prescribed by law, as he believed that while breaking an unjust law could be a moral duty, one must also be prepared to face its consequences. Rather than taking legal defence, he chose to set an example for every Indian. Although he was released unconditionally on 5 February 1924, after undergoing surgery on 12 January 1924, the British authorities imprisoned him multiple times in later years—after the Dandi March, for instance, and again following the Quit India Movement.

Despite being a trained barrister, Gandhi never participated in the Constituent Assembly debates, nor did he ever express a desire to hold political office. Although he could have easily become the first Prime Minister of India, he never aspired to any such post. In fact, Gandhi formally resigned from the primary membership of the Indian National Congress in 1934, choosing instead to focus on constructive work and village industries. Yet, he continued to exert immense influence in the Congress. On 15 August 1947, the day of India's independence, while the entire nation rejoiced and gathered in Delhi, Gandhi was in Calcutta, working to quell the communal violence that had engulfed the city.

In a determined effort to restore peace in Bengal, Gandhi undertook a fast that he vowed to continue until the violence ceased. As his health began to decline rapidly, public concern grew, and his moral appeal deeply impacted the warring communities. Ultimately, members of both Hindu and Muslim communities were moved to renounce violence and voluntarily surrendered their arms before Gandhi, prompting him to end his fast. Recognizing his efforts to bring peace in Bengal, Lord Mountbatten, the last British Viceroy, famously remarked:[15]

> In Punjab, we have 55,000 soldiers and large-scale rioting on our hands. In Bengal, our forces consist of one man, and there is no rioting [...] May I be allowed to pay my tribute to the one-man boundary force.

It is because of moments like these that Gandhi remains, in the eyes of many, the greatest Indian after Gautam Buddha, a man whose silent moral strength eclipsed the power of empires.

---

[15]Government of India, *The Collected Works of Mahatma Gandhi*, Vol. 89, 1 August 1947–10 November 1947, Publications Division, Ministry of Information and Broadcasting.

THREE

ALIPORE CONSPIRACY CASE

Young Aurobindo was polite, intelligent and reserved—much like the ideal British gentleman. Although born into a Bengali family, his father harboured a strong desire for his son to be raised in the British way. With that aim, he sent him to England at an early age. There, he earned prestigious scholarships and went on to study at Cambridge, aspiring to join the Indian Civil Services, just as his father had envisioned. He successfully cleared the highly competitive exam in his first attempt and secured a high rank, which promised a comfortable and respectable career.

However, the English-speaking Bengali youth lacked the necessary skills in horsemanship and struggled with riding—a critical part of the civil service training in England. As a result, he was disqualified from the programme. This rejection left a lasting impression on young Aurobindo's psyche, planting a deep sense of unease and disillusionment with the British system. Disheartened, he returned to India, a land that now felt unfamiliar to him. On the invitation of the Raja Sahib, he decided to settle in Baroda and took up the position of professor in a college there.

Meanwhile, his younger brother, Barin Ghose, who was born in England and thus technically not Indian by birth, had already come to India before Aurobindo. Barin had become deeply involved in revolutionary activities in Bengal. The British decision to partition Bengal had triggered a wave of resentment among Bengali masses, especially the youth. At Barin's request, Aurobindo eventually joined him in Bengal to contribute to the cause of India's freedom. Barin played a pivotal role in organizing these disenchanted young men, channelling their anger into a revolutionary movement. He and his followers believed that constitutional methods alone were inadequate for overthrowing British rule and that violence was a justified means to achieve independence. Undoubtedly, Barin and his movement had the moral and ideological support of Aurobindo.

After leaving his job as professor, Aurobindo started taking part in political activities and he attended many meetings of the Congress. There he met Lokmanya Tilak, who, having endured imprisonment, had already achieved national fame. Aurobindo found in Tilak an exceptional revolutionary spirit. Their meeting laid the foundation of a strong bond, as Aurobindo admired Tilak's disdain for the moderate, reformist approach of the Congress and resonated with his more assertive line of action in Deccan. This encounter marked the beginning of a profound friendship between these two towering nationalist leaders.

Aurobindo was the main accused in the famous Alipore Bomb Case or Alipore Conspiracy Case. Interestingly, Charles Porten Beachcroft, the Sessions Judge who presided over the Alipore Conspiracy Case, had once been Aurobindo's batchmate both at Cambridge and later in the Indian Civil Services (ICS). In fact, Aurobindo had ranked significantly higher than Beachcroft in the ICS examination. For Judge Beachcroft, seeing his former peer from Cambridge and fellow civil service candidate now standing before him as an accused was a moment filled with mixed emotions. He was well aware of Aurobindo's brilliance as a student and believed that had Aurobindo remained in the civil services, he could have been a valuable asset to the British administration in India.

The Alipore Conspiracy Case was one of the most significant and sensational trials of British India. It took place at a time when unrest in Bengal had reached its peak. This case became a pivotal moment in India's revolutionary struggle against British rule and brought widespread national recognition to Aurobindo Ghose, who would later emerge as a renowned spiritual leader. To fully understand the Alipore Conspiracy Case, it is essential to first examine the trial of Khudiram Bose, who, along with Prafulla Chaki, had attempted to assassinate Douglas Kingsford.

Trial of Khudiram Bose

Douglas Kingsford, the Chief Presidency Magistrate of Calcutta, who was widely regarded as a biased judge, was particularly harsh towards Indians. He gained notoriety for delivering severe punishments to young political activists in Bengal. On 16 June 1907, he sentenced Bhupendra Nath Dutt, the brother of Swami Vivekananda, to one year of rigorous imprisonment for writing an article 'Dispelling of Fear' in the *Jugantar* newspaper. Outraged by his actions, Bengal revolutionaries decided to take revenge on Kingsford. However, before their plan could be executed, he was transferred to Muzaffarpur as a District Judge. The task of assassinating him was assigned to Khudiram Bose and Prafulla Kumar Chaki, both of whom were very young at the time. In April 1908, the duo arrived in Muzaffarpur and conducted a detailed survey of Kingsford's routine. They observed that he regularly visited the British Club every evening and they also identified the carriage he used for travel.

It was decided that they would assassinate him on 30 April 1908, by throwing bombs at his carriage when he would be on his way back from the club. Tragically, on that day Mrs Kennedy and Ms Grace Kennedy, the wife and daughter of Mr Kennedy, a practising advocate at the Muzaffarpur court, left the club at around 8.30 p.m. after playing bridge with Kingsford. They were travelling in a carriage identical to the one used by Kingsford. As their carriage approached the spot where Khudiram and Prafulla lay in wait, the two young men sprang out from the shadows and hurled bombs, Khudiram throwing the first, and Prafulla, the second. The explosion killed both Mrs and Ms Kennedy.

Though Kingsford escaped, the incident sent shockwaves through the British administration. The youth of the attackers further intensified the sensation. In their haste, the revolutionaries left behind shoes and other clues at the scene, which led the police to deduce that two young Bengali men were responsible. A reward of ₹5,000 was announced for their capture. Khudiram Bose was apprehended the next day from Waini, about 25 km from Muzaffarpur, while Prafulla Kumar Chaki, when confronted by police at Mokama railway station on 1 May 1908, shot himself to avoid arrest.

Khudiram was brought back to Muzaffarpur for trial. He confessed before the Superintendent of Police that although his intended target was Kingsford, he had accidentally killed Mrs and Ms Kennedy. At just 18 years old, Khudiram Bose became a celebrated figure in the history of India's revolutionary movement, remembered for his courage and youthful defiance against colonial rule. His trial started before the Muzaffarpur Court on 22 May 1908. Although Khudiram Bose pleaded guilty to the charge of murder before the court, the Sessions Judge, after recording his plea, decided to proceed with the trial and examine the evidence. The case was tried with the assistance of assessor[16] rather than a jury. Both assessors unanimously found the accused guilty of murder.

The Sessions Judge, Muzaffarpur, on 13 June 1908 concurred with their opinion, convicted Khudiram of the offence under Section 302 of the Indian Penal Code and sentenced him to death. On the advice of his advocate (Mr Kalidas Basu), Khudiram Bose filed an appeal against his conviction before the Calcutta High Court although he knew death was inevitable. A bench of Justice H.L. Bell and Justice Alfred Edward dismissed the appeal of Khudiram Bose on 13 July 1908 by observing that:[17]

> **48.** The accused is not a mere youth but a young man who has attained the age fixed for majority in this country. The crime was not committed at the instigation of older men present on the spot. For twenty days the accused and his companion had been in Muzaffarpur watching for an opportunity to commit the crime, and when they thought the opportunity offered itself, they carried it out with deliberation and determination after first taking

---

[16] In colonial India, assessors were individuals who assisted judges in criminal trials, especially in the Sessions Court, but they were not jurors. Their role was somewhat similar to lay judges or advisors, and they were part of the legal system during the British era under the Code of Criminal Procedure, 1898.

[17] 'Calcutta High Court: Khudiram Bose vs Emperor on 13 July 1908', *Indiankanoon*, https://tinyurl.com/5n8s8es2. Accessed on 6 January 2026.

precautions to avoid detection and secure escape. It is impossible to treat the accused as a young man who did not know fully well the serious nature of the crime, he was committing.

49. His confession does not appear to us to disclose that his feelings were undeveloped or that the act was one of criminal folly. He has given his reasons for the commission of the crime and has explained the steps which he took to carry it into effect in concert with his companion. His conduct may, as the learned pleader observed, indicate great depravity and wickedness of mind, but that is not a fact which could be taken into consideration in extenuation of the offence.

50. Nowhere in the defence during the trial was it stated that the accused was a tool in the hands of others. In his confession he claimed that the intention to commit the crime was his own, though it had been aroused by the speeches and writings of others and that the commission of the crime was carried out by him and Dinesh at their own initiative. Whether this be true or not it is impossible for us to say, but on the materials before us we are unable to give effect to the suggestion of the learned pleader that the accused was a mere tool in the hands of others in committing the crime.

51. The murder was deliberately planned and cruelly carried out under cover of darkness by the accused and his companion, both being armed with pistols and having made careful preparations for their own safety and escape.

> **52.** We can find in the case no extenuating circumstance which would in law justify our interference with the extreme sentence which has been passed on the accused by the Sessions Judge. We, therefore, confirm the conviction and sentence, and dismiss the appeal.

Khudiram Bose was ultimately executed on 11 August 1908, at the young age of 18.

Revolutionary Activities of the Ghose Brothers

Barindra Ghose was another accused in the conspiracy case. After coming to India, Barin spent some time in Bengal, focusing on recruiting men for organizing the revolutionary movement. In Bengal, with Barin's assistance, Aurobindo Ghose established contacts and inspired revolutionaries such as Bagha Jatin (Jatindranath Mukherjee) and Surendranath Tagore.[18]

Aurobindo, along with his brother, also helped found several youth clubs in Bengal, including the Anushilan Samiti[19] of Calcutta in 1902. Many young men who joined organizations like the Anushilan Samiti were motivated to pursue physical training, participate in parades and receive martial instruction, often becoming highly skilled in stick-fighting (*lathi khela*). In 1907, following Barin's suggestion, Aurobindo agreed to launch a Bengali newspaper, *Jugantar*, which openly promoted revolutionary action and the total rejection of British rule,

---

[18]Surendranath Tagore was the nephew of Rabindranath Tagore.

[19]The Anushilan Samiti was a revolutionary organization that emerged in early 20th century Bengal with the goal of ending British rule in India through armed struggle. Initially a network of fitness clubs (*akharas*), it evolved into an underground society that used bombings and assassinations to fight for independence.

including publishing articles that provided guidance on guerrilla warfare. Barindra was convinced that a solely political movement would not suffice, and he stressed the importance of preparing people for armed revolution.

Convinced that political assassinations were a necessary response to severe repression, Barin championed this method, despite knowing that it alone could not achieve independence. Meanwhile, Aurobindo, through his articles in the English daily *Bande Mataram*, propagated the ideals of nationalism, complete independence, national education, etc. He also outlined strategies for mass movements, such as promoting swadeshi and passive resistance, while sharply criticizing British rule and the British character.

The revolutionaries operating under the leadership of Barindra Ghose initially targeted Sir Andrew Fraser, the Lieutenant Governor of Bengal. Their plan was to bomb the train carrying him on the night of 6 December 1907; however, the attempt was unsuccessful. Their second target was L. Tardivel, the Mayor of Chandernagore. This attempt too ended in failure. The third target was Douglas Kingsford, the Chief Presidency Magistrate of Calcutta. For this mission, Barindra Ghose selected Prafulla Chaki and Khudiram Bose, directing them to proceed to Muzaffarpur. The Muzaffarpur bomb-throwing incident, as we are aware, eventually became the catalyst for the Alipore Bomb Case. The Alipore Bomb Case was the most sensational trial of his time, drawing tremendous attention from both British and Indian media.

Unravelling of the Alipore Conspiracy Case

During the investigation into the murders of Mrs and Ms Kennedy, the police uncovered the existence of secret revolutionary societies in Bengal, committed to achieving freedom through violent means. This discovery led the authorities to believe that the murders were part of a larger conspiracy. Consequently, several Bengali youths were arrested on charges of conspiracy, marking the beginning of what came to be known as the Alipore Conspiracy Case. The principal accused in the Alipore Conspiracy Case, as mentioned earlier, were Aurobindo Ghose and his brother, Barin, whom the British government was determined to prosecute at any cost.

THE TRIAL

King-Emperor v. Barindra Kumar Ghosh & Ors.
From 19 October 1908 to 14 April 1909
Judgment on 6 May 1909

Judge: Charles Porten Beachcroft I.C.S.

Leading Counsel for the Prosecution: Mr Eardley Norton & Ashutosh Biswas

Leading Counsel for the Accused: Chittaranjan Das (C.R. Das) & R.C. Banerjee

Following the murders of Mrs and Ms Kennedy, widespread police raids commenced on 2 May 1908. During these operations, the police arrested Barindra Ghose along with seventeen others from 32, Muraripukur Garden House—the epicentre of revolutionary activities in Bengal—jointly owned by Barindra Ghose and Aurobindo Ghose.

The Muraripukur estate in Manicktolla (North Calcutta) served as an 'ashram for revolutionary sannyasins', where under Barindra's leadership, young recruits followed a distinctive regimen that included meditation, the study of the Gita and Upanishads, lessons in Indian history and international revolutionary movements, physical exercises, wrestling, stick-fighting, and training in military tactics and the use of firearms.

Aurobindo Ghose was arrested and placed in solitary confinement at the Alipore Jail, viewed by the authorities as the principal strategist behind the bomb conspiracy and the secret activities of the Anushilan Samiti. During the raids, the police recovered arms, ammunition, explosives and documentary evidence supporting the existence of a revolutionary conspiracy. The raids continued throughout the month, leading to further arrests. In addition to Muraripukur, several other locations across Calcutta were raided, resulting in more revolutionaries being taken into custody. On 18 May 1908, the case was brought before the Committing Magistrate, Mr Birley, I.C.S., at Alipore, who subsequently committed the following individuals to the Sessions Court under Sections 121,[20] 121A,[21] 123[22] and 124 of the Indian Penal Code.

---

[20]Section 121 of the Indian Penal Code (IPC) deals with the offence of waging, attempting to wage, or abetting the waging of war against the Government of India (formerly Crown).

[21]121A of IPC refers to the Indian Penal Code section that deals with conspiracy to commit offences punishable under Section 121.

[22]Section 123 of IPC penalizes concealing a design to wage war against the Government of India (formerly Crown) with the intention of facilitating it.

Sr. No.	*Name of Accused*	*Sr. No.*	*Name of Accused*
1	Barindra Kumar Ghose	19	Sailendra Nath Bose
2	Indra Bhusan Rai	20	Dindayal Bose
3	Ullaskar Dutta	21	Sudhir Kumar Sirker
4	Upendra Nath Banerji	22	Krishna Jiban Sanyal
5	Sisir Kumar Ghose	23	Hrishi Kesh Kanjilal
6	Nalini Kanta Sircar Gupta	24	Birendra Nath Ghose
7	Sachindra K. Sen	25	Dharani Nath Gupta
8	Paresh Chandra Maullik	26	Nagendra Nath Gupta
9	Kunjal Lal Sah	27	Ashok Chandra Nandi
10	Bijoy Kumar Nag	28	Susil Kumar Sen
11	Narendra Nath Bakshi	29	Birendra Chandra Sen
12	Purna Chandra Sen	30	Hem. Chandra Sen
13	Hemendra Nath Ghose	31	Debabrata Bose
14	Bibhuti Bhusan Sarker	32	Indra Nath Nandy
15	Nirapada Roy	33	Nikhileswar Roy Mullick
16	Hem Chandra Das	34	Bijoy Ch. Bhattacharjee
17	Arabinda Ghose[23]	35	Bal Kissen Hari Kani
18	Abinash Ch. Bhattacharji	36	Provash Chandra Deb

Murder of Approver or King's Witness

During the early hearings in Magistrate's Court, Naren Goswami (former member of Anushilan Samiti), who became

---

[23]Arabinda Ghose refers to Aurobindo Ghosh, the historical figure. This spelling has been used in legal documentation.

a government witness in return for a full pardon, testified that Aurobindo Ghose was aware of all the dacoities and bombings planned by the Samiti and was actively involved in their planning. He further stated that Aurobindo was the *Boro Karta* (Principal Leader) of the Secret Society, while his younger brother Barin served as the *Chhoto Karta* (Deputy Leader). Fearing retaliation from his former associates, prison authorities transferred Naren Goswami to the jail block designated for European prisoners.

Kanailal Dutt and Satyendra Nath Bose, both accused in the Alipore Bomb Case, were admitted to the Jail Hospital as patients. Satyendra sent a message to Naren Goswami, who had already become a government witness, pretending he too wanted to turn approver. When Naren came to the hospital to meet him, the three went to the verandah for a private conversation. Suddenly, Kanai and Satyendra pulled out their revolvers, which had been smuggled into the jail for a planned escape. Naren tried to flee but was chased by Kanai and Satyen. During the pursuit, nine shots were fired. A shot from Kanai's revolver fatally wounded Naren, who fell on the ground and died instantly.

Kanailal and Satyendra were quickly found guilty and sentenced to death by hanging. Legally, Naren Goswami's testimony before the magistrate's court, which now could not be cross-examined by the accused/defence, became inadmissible in the Sessions Court. By eliminating Naren, Kanailal and Satyendra ensured that his potentially damaging statements against Aurobindo Ghose and other revolutionaries could not be used, effectively safeguarding Aurobindo and others from serious legal consequences.

Story of a Sweet Letter

The British government was determined to implicate Aurobindo at any cost. To achieve this, they fabricated various pieces of evidence intended to link him to the conspiracy. The most crucial among these was a 'sweet letter', which, according to the prosecution, was written by Barin to his brother Aurobindo. The prosecution placed significant emphasis on this letter to establish Aurobindo's connection to the alleged assassination plots. They believed that if the court accepted the letter as genuine, it would decisively confirm Aurobindo's guilt. Below is a reproduction of the content of the so-called 'sweet letter':[24]

> Dear Brother 27th December, 1907
>
> Now is the time. Please try and make them meet for our conference. We must have sweets all over India, ready for emergencies. I wait here for your answer.
>
> Your affectionate
> Barindra K Ghose

The suggestion of the prosecution was that 'sweet' meant bombs. Judge Beachcroft rejected this suggestion and did not consider the letter genuine. Some apparent anomalies like Barin addressing his elder brother as 'Dear Brother' instead of '*Sej-da*' which was his usual form of address, writing his full name instead of writing the first name, writing to Aurobindo a formal letter when they were staying at the same place and meeting each other off and on, spelling errors, were some of the unusual points about the letter. These major inconsistencies

---

[24]Samanta, Amiya K. (ed.), *Alipore Bomb Trial, 1908-1910*, Frontpage Publications, Kolkata, 2018.

made the provenance of the letter doubtful and in this context the defence lawyer raised the possibility of the letter being forged.[25]

Conclusion of Trial

The prosecution presented 206 witnesses and submitted 1,438 exhibits over the course of the trial. Nearly all the accused, including Aurobindo and his brother, faced charges of 'conspiracy' or 'waging war against the King'—offences equivalent to high treason and punishable by death. The prosecution was led by Eardley Norton, one of the leading barristers of the Madras Presidency, while Chittaranjan Das[26] appeared and argued on behalf of Aurobindo Ghose. When the court asked Aurobindo Ghose whether he wished to make any statement, he replied that he would leave the matter to his lawyer, who would speak on his behalf, and that he himself did not wish to make any statement or respond to the court's questions. If any statement attributed to him existed, he clarified, it must have been prepared by his lawyer and not personally made by him. C.R. Das's arguments in favour of Aurobindo in the Sessions Court spanned eight days, culminating in the following powerful and passionate concluding address:[27]

---

[25]Ibid.

[26]Chittaranjan Das (C.R. Das), popularly known as Deshbandhu, was a prominent Bengali freedom fighter, political activist and lawyer in early twentieth-century India. He played a major role in the Indian independence movement.

[27]Samanta, Amiya K. (ed.), *Alipore Bomb Trial, 1908-1910*, Frontpage Publications, Kolkata, 2018.

> My appeal to you therefore is that a man like this who is being charged with the offences imputed to him stands not only before the bar in this Court but stands before the bar of the High Court of History and my appeal to you is this: That long after this controversy is hushed in silence, long after this turmoil, this agitation ceases, long after he is dead and gone, he will be looked upon as the poet of patriotism, as the prophet of nationalism and the lover of humanity. Long after he is dead and gone, his words will be echoed and re-echoed not only in India, but across distant seas and lands. Therefore, I say that the man in his position is not only standing before the bar of this Court but before the bar of the High Court of History.

The Judgment Day

In light of the widespread public support following the executions of Khudiram Bose, Kanailal Dutta and Satyen Bose, the date of the verdict was kept a secret. Additional security measures were enforced, with a reserve force of European officers placed on standby to respond to any potential outbreak of violence or unrest in the streets of Calcutta.[28] Amidst this heightened security, Sessions Judge Charles P. Beachcroft delivered his verdict on 6 May 1909 in Alipore Sessions Court. The first verdict was pronounced against Barindra Ghose and Ullaskar Dutt. Notably, Barindra had been born in England and brought to India when he was just a year old. Under British Indian law, he was given the option to be tried as a

[28]'Aurobindo Ghosh and Alipore Bomb Case', *Alipore Museum*, https://tinyurl.com/4pc32u5y. Accessed on 6 January 2026.

British citizen. However, Barin, true to his nationalist ideals, firmly declined.

In his judgment, Sessions Judge C.P. Beachcroft found both Barindra Ghose and Ullaskar Dutt guilty under Section 121 of waging war against the King and sentenced them both to death. Both filed an appeal before the Calcutta High Court challenging their conviction, which ultimately resulted in their sentences being commuted to life imprisonment. They were deported to the Cellular Jail in the Andamans, where they remained incarcerated until a general amnesty was declared in 1920. Some of the accused in the trial were sentenced to ten years' imprisonment, while others received seven years of imprisonment, and 17 of the accused were acquitted.

The verdict for Aurobindo was announced last. Judge C.P. Beachcroft noted that while there was substantial evidence against many accused, very little directly linked Aurobindo to the conspiracy. The prosecution had failed in its attempt to depict Aurobindo as part of the group, even as its leader. After Naren Goswami's assassination, there was very little evidence connecting Aurobindo to Barin's group besides his published views in *Bande Mataram* and *Jugantar*. C.R. Das successfully argued that Aurobindo's writings on independence were aligned with the philosophical ideals of liberty long embraced by English intellectuals. In his judgment, Judge C.P. Beachcroft, acquitting Aurobindo, remarked:[29]

> I now come to the case of Aurobindo Ghose, the most important accused in the case. He is the accused, whom more than any other the prosecution are anxious to have

[29]Samanta, Amiya K. (ed.), *Alipore Bomb Trial, 1908-1910*, Frontpage Publications, Kolkata, 2018.

> convicted and but for his presence in the dock there is no doubt that the case would have been finished long ago. It is partly for that reason that I have left his case till last of all and partly because the case against him depends to a very great extent, in fact almost entirely, upon association with other accused persons
>
> [...] The point is whether his writings & speeches which in themselves seem to advocate nothing more than the regeneration of his country, taken with the facts proved against him in this case are sufficient to show that he was a member of the conspiracy. And taking all the evidence together I am of opinion that it falls short of such proof as would justify me in finding him guilty of so serious a charge.

Aftermath of the Alipore Conspiracy Case

The incarceration of several prominent leaders of the Anushilan Samiti led to a decline in the influence and activities of its Manicktolla branch. Its operations were soon overshadowed by the emergence of the Jugantar branch, led by Bagha Jatin. During his time in jail, Aurobindo Ghose underwent profound spiritual experiences and realizations, which radically transformed his outlook on life.[30] His aspirations expanded beyond merely serving or liberating the nation. After being acquitted by the court, Aurobindo relocated to Pondicherry, then a French colony, where he spent the rest of his life and founded his Ashram. Meanwhile, the revolutionaries associated with the secret society remained determined to

[30]'Aurobindo Ghosh and Alipore Bomb Case', *Alipore Museum*, https://tinyurl.com/4pc32u5y. Accessed on 6 January 2026.

exact retribution against the British authorities and their collaborators involved in the Alipore Conspiracy Case.

Their first act of vengeance targeted Inspector Nandalal Banerjee, who had pursued Prafulla Chaki at Mokama Railway Station, an encounter that led Prafulla to take his own life. Revolutionary Srish Pal avenged this act by shooting Banerjee dead on 9 November 1908, shortly after the trial concluded.

The second target was Ashutosh Biswas, the public prosecutor in the Alipore case, who had played a crucial role in securing several convictions and was perceived as having insulted the revolutionaries during the trial proceedings. Revolutionary Charu Chandra Bose undertook the task. Despite having a crippled right hand, he managed to steady the gun and, firing with his left hand, shot Biswas on 10 February 1909, in a courtroom filled with police officers.

The third and final target was the notorious Shamsul Alam, the chief investigating officer in the Alipore case. Biren Datta Gupta accepted the responsibility of eliminating him. On 24 January 1910, in broad daylight, within the corridors of the Calcutta High Court, Biren shot Shamsul Alam at point-blank range. He attempted to escape while firing his revolver but was apprehended by court guards after exhausting his ammunition. Biren Datta Gupta was subsequently hanged on 21 February 1910 at the Alipore Presidency Jail.

FOUR

TRIAL OF BAL GANGADHAR TILAK

A tense silence gripped the courtroom. The dim glow of the gas lamps added to the charged atmosphere, intensifying the unease in the already charged room. Outside, it rained steadily, and from time to time, the crack of thunder pierced the stillness within. It was an unusual sitting, extending late into the night; the court remained in session until 9.30 p.m. All eyes were fixed on the door, awaiting the return of the nine-member jury, who were to deliver their verdict. Bal Gangadhar Tilak, the accused, stood charged under Sections 153A and 124A of the Indian Penal Code, for offences relating to promoting enmity and sedition.

Having argued his own defence tirelessly over six consecutive days, Tilak was hoping that he would be acquitted. A revered nationalist and editor of the widely circulated Marathi weekly printed in Poona and also distributed in Bombay, *Kesari*, Tilak also served as its publisher and printer. Two of his articles in *Kesari*, 'The Country's Misfortune' (12 May 1908) and 'These Remedies Are Not Lasting' (9 June 1908),[31] had alarmed the British administration. Stung by his words, the colonial government

[31]Please see *Appendix 3* for reference.

appeared determined to imprison him on the charge of sedition. At approximately 9:30 p.m., the jury, comprising seven European and two Indian members, returned to the courtroom with their verdict. Addressing the jury through the foreman[32], Clerk of the Crown asked: 'Gentlemen, are you unanimous?'

Foreman: 'No.'

Clerk: 'How are you divided?'

Foreman: 'Seven to two.'

Clerk: 'Is that division applicable to all charges?'

Foreman: 'Yes, on all the charges.'

Justice Dinshaw Davar who was presiding the court then turned to the foreman and enquired:

Justice Dinshaw Davar: 'Mr Foreman, is there any possibility of the jury reaching a unanimous verdict?'

Foreman: 'I regret to say, my Lord, there is none.'

Justice Davar: 'No possibility at all?'

Foreman: 'No chance.'

Davar then turned to the accused, Bal Gangadhar Tilak, and asked, since he had been declared guilty by the jury, whether he wished to make any final statement before the order on sentence was passed. In response, what Tilak said will always be remembered in history as a powerful articulation of his nationalist conviction. Tilak said:[33]

---

[32]The foreman is the spokesperson and leader of the jury in a jury trial.

[33]Kelkar, N.C., *Full and Authentic Report of the Tilak Trial*, N.C. Kelkar, Bombay, 1908.

> All I wish to say is that in spite of the verdict of the Jury, I maintain that I am innocent. There are higher Powers that rule the destiny of things and it may be the will of the Providence that the cause which I represent may prosper more by my suffering than by my remaining free.

The trial of Bal Gangadhar Tilak began on 13 July 1908 during the third criminal session of the Bombay High Court and continued until 22 July 1908. This was not Tilak's first encounter with sedition charges; in 1897, he had already been convicted under the same provision of the Indian Penal Code by the same court and was sentenced to 18 months' imprisonment.

An interesting fact is that Mr Dinshaw Davar, who had served as Tilak's defence counsel during the 1897 trial, now presided as the judge in the 1908 proceedings. The jury comprised nine members, including two Indians, who returned a verdict of 'not guilty', while the remaining seven European jurors found Tilak 'guilty'. Based on this 7–2 majority verdict, Justice Davar sentenced Tilak to six years of imprisonment in Burma along with a fine of ₹1,000.

THE TRIAL

Emperor v. Bal Gangadhar Tilak

(Case No. 16 & 17 of 1908)

In The High Court of Judicature at Bombay

On 24 June 1908, Bal Gangadhar Tilak was arrested from Sardar Griha in Bombay, where he was residing at the time. He was produced the following day, 25 June 1908, before Mr A.H.S. Aston, the Chief Presidency Magistrate, Bombay, who denied him bail and remanded him to judicial custody.

On 29 June 1908, after recording some preliminary evidence, Mr Aston committed Tilak to stand trial in the Third Criminal Session of the Bombay High Court under Sections 124A and 153A of the Indian Penal Code.

Subsequently, on 2 July 1908, Mr Mohammad Ali Jinnah appeared on Tilak's behalf and argued for bail before Justice Dinshaw Davar. However, the application for bail was rejected. In a notable contrast, during Tilak's first sedition trial in 1897, Justice Badruddin Tyabji had granted him bail and his order was later hailed as a landmark ruling in the evolution of bail jurisprudence, especially in sedition cases. Ironically, Justice Davar's refusal to grant bail in the second sedition case went on to be frequently cited in legal discourse as a precedent for rejection of bail in serious political offences.

Arguments for the Prosecution

Bal Gangadhar Tilak was charged under Sections 124A and 153A of the Indian Penal Code for two articles published in *Kesari*. The first charge was under Section 124A IPC (sedition). The British government argued that this provision allowed individuals to freely criticize governmental actions, but it did not permit the use of the press as a means to defame or incite hatred against the government. It further argued that while constructive criticism on administrative measures was protected, the law prohibited assertions such as the government had acted with malice or in disregard of public interest, particularly if such remarks fuelled animosity between rulers and the ruled. According to the prosecution, through his aforesaid articles in *Kesari*, Bal Gangadhar Tilak created hatred and contempt against the British government and community.

The first article, titled 'The Country's Misfortune', was written by Tilak in the context of the Muzaffarpur bomb case, where two British women were killed due to a bomb allegedly intended for a government official. Tilak's article blamed the British government for creating the conditions that had led to such violence, portraying its rule as tyrannical and self-serving. Tilak had written in his article that the British government was driven solely by self-interest, moderated only by the fear of public backlash. The prosecution argued that such statements constituted defamation of the Government of India and of Great Britain. More importantly Tilak in his aforesaid article called for power to be transferred from British hands to Indians, advocating for 'Swarajya', a term he used to mean self-rule or independence.

In his second article, titled 'These Remedies Are Not Lasting', Tilak, according to the prosecution, allegedly suggested that the government could not stop the manufacture of bombs, which he described as easy to make using simple chemicals. The prosecution argued that such remarks constituted incitement, encouraging readers to engage in violent resistance. Moreover, the article also implied that other nations had secured their freedom through similar means (by using bombs) and that India could do the same. He accused the British administration of 'selfish governance', suggesting that it enriched England at the expense of India. Prosecution argued that under Section 153A IPC, it was an offence to publish material that promoted enmity between different communities, particularly on racial grounds, and Tilak's repeated references to the British as 'white' and 'alien rulers' in his article were deliberate attempts to inflame racial animosity between the native Indian population and their European rulers.

From a legal and historical point of view, the way the British government argued this case before the Bombay High Court shows how sensitive the British colonial government was to any political criticism or dissent that was based on nationalist thoughts. It also shows how the law on sedition was used as a tool to punish and suppress the growing support for India's freedom movement especially when those ideas were shared through popular newspapers in local languages.

After the prosecution concluded its arguments and presented its evidence, it was Bal Gangadhar Tilak's turn to present his defence. Unlike the British government, Tilak did not call any witnesses on his behalf. Instead, he chose to argue his case personally, addressing the court and jury for six consecutive days. It is worth noting that Tilak was highly educated and articulate, having obtained his law degree in 1880. He began his defence speech at around 4 p.m. on Wednesday, 15 July 1908, and continued until Wednesday, 22 July 1908, excluding Saturday and Sunday. His arguments in court were indeed historic and constitute a very important piece of literary and legal work. For the benefit of our readers, we present a summary of Tilak's key arguments in the following paragraphs:

Summary of Mr Tilak's Statements before the Jury

Tilak began his defence by arguing that innuendos and accusations cannot be fairly drawn from the translated versions of the articles presented in court. He contended that the articles, allegedly authored by him, were not placed before the jury in their original form, and that the translations had distorted their meaning. According to Tilak, any allegations based on such flawed translations were inherently unreliable.

Tilak emphasized that the question of his intent was central to the case and argued that the articles, read in isolation and through imperfect translation, could not serve as a fair basis to determine guilt or innocence. He cautioned the jury that it would be both unjust and dangerous to judge him guilty merely because certain words distorted through faulty translation appeared to provoke hatred or contempt, especially within a community about which the jury had limited understanding. To illustrate his point, Tilak offered a hypothetical analogy: suppose the jury were asked to pass judgment on an article originally written in French, translated into English, and then to assess the effect that article might have on the French-speaking population in England, that task would clearly be fraught with the risk of misinterpretation.

Tilak contended that the articles in question were originally written in Marathi and intended specifically for a Marathi-speaking audience. He urged the jury to consider the impact these writings might have on the minds of Marathi readers who understood the language and cultural context before they formed any opinion.

Tilak further argued that the prosecution had failed to fulfil its responsibility and had improperly shifted the burden of proof onto the defence. He argued that it was the duty of the British government to establish, through credible evidence, that the author had crossed the boundaries of fair expression, legitimate criticism and reasonable dissent.

Tilak once again used an illustration to make his point. He argued that if the government were to appoint an officer to investigate the causes of public unrest, and that officer submitted a report stating that the unrest stemmed from specific grievances that the government could easily address, it would be unreasonable to accuse the officer of disaffection. The officer would merely be describing existing public sentiment and relaying it to the government, not inciting or aggravating it. Tilak maintained that to 'excite feelings of disaffection' under Section 124A of the Indian Penal Code, an individual must either intensify existing discontent or create such feelings where none existed. However, simply reporting or expressing already existing public emotions does not constitute sedition. On that basis, Tilak argued that his writings were reflective of prevailing societal conditions and that he, like the hypothetical officer, was not promoting disaffection but merely articulating it.

Tilak submitted that the British government had not presented any evidence before the jury indicating that his writings had caused discontent in any part of the state. He emphasized that the articles in question were written as part of his patriotic duty, with the intention of serving the nation, and not to incite violence or provoke unrest among the people.

Tilak argued that the liberties enjoyed by Anglo-Indians in India should equally be available to Indian citizens, as they too were subjects of the British Empire. He questioned before the jury why an Indian subject in India should not be entitled to the same freedoms that were granted to British subjects in England or to Anglo-Indians residing in India. Tilak asserted that he had every right to express his views to the government, as well as to represent the opinions and concerns of his community on such matters.

Tilak further argued that the bureaucracy did not constitute the government itself, and therefore, criticizing the bureaucracy could not be equated with inciting hatred or contempt against the government established by law. On this basis, he contended that the charge under Section 124A of the Indian Penal Code was not applicable, as his writings were directed solely at the bureaucratic machinery, not at the government as a whole.

Tilak further contended that he had never instigated people to manufacture bombs through his writings. The suggestion that he had done so was, according to him, a misinterpretation propagated by Anglo-Indian newspapers. He clarified that he did not support bomb-throwing, nor did he regard it as anything less than a criminal and condemnable act. However, he argued that while condemning such violence, it was also necessary to equally denounce the repressive actions of the government that might have contributed to public unrest.

In conclusion, Tilak acknowledged that certain prejudices might exist against him among the jury members, but he earnestly appealed to them to set aside such biases and to assess his case solely on the basis of facts and evidence. He assured the court that he had concealed nothing and had clearly explained the intent behind the publication of the articles. Reiterating his belief in the fairness of the judicial process, he expressed confidence that, upon considering all the circumstances, the jury would return a verdict of not guilty. His final words to the jury before concluding his submission were:[34]

> Gentlemen, that He (God) before whom all of us will have to stand one day and render an account of our actions will inspire you with the courage of your convictions and help you in arriving at a right decision on the issue involved in this case.

[34]Ibid.

Judgment Day

Justice Dinshaw Davar of the Bombay High Court sentenced Bal Gangadhar Tilak to six years of imprisonment, to be served in Burma, along with a fine of ₹1,000. While pronouncing the sentence, Justice Davar made several harsh observations about Tilak's actions. He remarked:[35]

> It is my painful duty now to pass sentence upon you. I cannot tell you how painful it is to me to see you in this position. You are a man of undoubted talents and great power and influence. Those talents and that influence, if used for the good of your country would have been instrumental in bringing about a great deal of happiness for those very people whose cause you espouse. Ten years ago, you were convicted and the court dealt most leniently with you then, and the Crown dealt still more kindly with you. After you had undergone your imprisonment for one year, six months of the sentence was remitted upon conditions which you accepted- The condition which you signed then was this. (Reads from document- "I hereby accept and agree to the above conditions, understanding the meaning to be such act or writing as is considered as an offence.") It seems to me that it must be a diseased mind, a most perverted mind that could say that the articles which you have written are legitimate weapons in political agitation. They are seething with sedition; they preach violence; they speak of murders with approval and the cowardly and atrocious act of committing murders with bombs not only seems to meet with your approval but

[35]Ibid.

you hail the advent of the bomb in India as if something has come to India for its good. As I said it can only be a diseased and perverted mind that can think that bombs are legitimate instruments in political agitations. And it would be a diseased mind that could ever have thought that the articles you wrote were articles that could have been legitimately written. Your hatred of the ruling class has not disappeared during these ten years. And these were deliberately and definitely written week by week, not, as you say, on the spur of the moment but a fortnight after that cruel and cowardly outrage had been committed upon two innocent Englishwomen. You wrote about bombs as if they were legitimate instruments in political agitations. Such journalism is a curse to the country. I feel much sorrow in sentencing you. I have considered most anxiously in the case of a verdict of guilty being returned against you what sentence I should pass upon you. And I decided to pass a sentence which I considered will be stigmatized as what is called 'misplaced leniency' I do not think I can pass, consistently with my duty and consistently with the offence of which you have been found guilty, a lighter sentence than I am going to give you- And I think for a man in your position and circumstances that sentence will vindicate the law and meet the ends of justice. You are liable to be transported for life under the first two charges. I have considered whether to sentence you to transportation or imprisonment. Having regard to your age and other circumstances I think it is most desirable in the interest of peace and order, and it the interest of the country which you profess to love, that you should be out of it for some time. Under Section 124A

> I am entitled to pass sentence of transportation for life or any short period, and I pass a sentence of three years' transportation under each of the first two charges, the sentence to run consecutively. You will thus have six years', transportation. On the third charge which is punishable not by transportation but by fine or imprisonment I do not think I will add to your troubles any additional period of imprisonment. I therefore fine you Rs. 1000.

Aftermath

Despite heavy rain and the hearing extending late into the night until 10.00 p.m., thousands had gathered outside the Bombay High Court, anxiously waiting to hear the fate of their beloved leader. Lokmanya Bal Gangadhar Tilak was the most prominent Maratha nationalist of his time. Following the pronouncement of the sentence, Tilak was escorted by the police through the rear exit, as a massive crowd had assembled at the main gate hoping to catch a glimpse of their leader. While passing through the court's corridor under heavy security, Tilak noticed Junior Davar (son of Justice Dinshaw Davar) who had served as his defence counsel in the lower court. The young advocate appeared visibly uncomfortable, perhaps due to the fact that it was his own father, Justice Dinshaw Davar, who had just sentenced Tilak to six years of imprisonment. Sensing his discomfort, Tilak paused briefly, offered his thanks for Davar's professional efforts, and then continued on his way. In the aftermath of Tilak's sentencing, riots broke out in parts of the city, prompting the military to be called in. Tragically, fifteen people lost their lives and many others were injured in the violence that followed.

FIVE

TRIAL OF BHAGAT SINGH

Bara Singh, the *chowkidar* of the Firoz Shah Tughlaq Fort near ITO in Delhi, was on his usual round of the fort when he spotted some young men gathered there, including a young Sikh. They seemed to be engaged in a hushed, secretive conversation. Finding their behaviour suspicious, Bara Singh observed them for a while before approaching and asking them what they were doing. On being asked, the Sikh man replied that they were studying together for their upcoming examination. Although Bara Singh knew this to be untrue, he merely nodded and walked away.

These young men were no ordinary students, nor were they preparing for any exam. They were young revolutionaries plotting to overthrow the British imperial government and win freedom for their motherland. It was during this very meeting that Bhagat Singh (who was the Sikh young man whom Bara Singh had seen) and his comrades resolved to form the Hindustan Socialist Republican Association (HSRA), dedicated to waging an armed revolution in India. Bara Singh would later be called as one of the 457 prosecution witnesses in the Lahore Conspiracy Case, a historic trial aimed at proving charges of conspiracy and murder against Bhagat Singh, Rajguru, Sukhdev and twenty-two other accused.

During his lifetime, Bhagat Singh faced two prominent trials, one for throwing bombs in the Central Legislative Assembly (old Parliament building), Delhi, and the other for conspiring and assassinating the Assistant Superintendent of Police (ACP) Mr Saunders in Lahore, the latter incident being famously known as the Lahore Conspiracy Case.

The first trial, commonly referred to as the Assembly Bomb Case, commenced in 1929, in which charges under Section 307 of the Indian Penal Code (attempt to murder) were brought against Bhagat Singh and Batukeshwar Datta. While investigating this case, the police launched a separate probe into Bhagat Singh and his associates under Sections 121 and 121A (waging war and conspiracy to wage war). Later, when evidence emerged linking Bhagat Singh to the killing of Mr Saunders, Section 302 (murder) was also added to the charges.

THE FIRST TRIAL: ASSEMBLY BOMB CASE

Crown v. Bhagat Singh and Batukeshwar Datta
Session Trial No. 9 of 1929
Decided on 12 June 1929

Charge: Section 307 of Indian Penal Code and Section 3 of the Explosive Substances Act, 1908

Prosecutor: Rai Bahadur Suryanarayan

Counsel for Accused: Asaf Ali[36]

Session Judge: Leonard Middleton

[36]Asaf Ali was a prominent Congress leader.

Facts of the Case

On 8 April 1929, Bhagat Singh and Batukeshwar Dutt threw harmless, low-intensity bombs inside the Central Legislative Assembly to protest against the passing of the Public Safety Bill[37] and the Trade Disputes Bill.[38] Their intention was not to harm anyone but to draw public attention to the unjust and discriminatory nature of these laws. Bhagat Singh's bomb landed on the floor of the House in a narrow gangway, causing minor injuries to some members of the Assembly. Batukeshwar Dutt then threw a second bomb, which damaged several empty seats. Following the explosions, both revolutionaries scattered handmade pamphlets inside the Assembly chamber. Bhagat Singh and Batukeshwar Dutt immediately surrendered and did not try to escape as they had realized that their arrest would also serve the purpose for which they were fighting.

Sardar Sobha Singh (father of famous writer Khushwant Singh) was one of the most important witnesses of the prosecution in this case and he deposed before the court that he had seen Bhagat Singh standing in the gallery and throwing something which looked like a cigarette case and this act was followed by the noise of an explosion and the appearance of smoke.

---

[37]This Bill was brought to curb revolutionary activities in India and gave unrestricted right to the police to arrest anyone without normal legal safeguards.

[38]The Trade Disputes Bill was brought to curb the right of factory or industrial workers to strike.

Findings of the Court

The Sessions Judge of Delhi, Mr Leonard Middleton, convicted Bhagat Singh and Batukeshwar Dutt under Section 307 of the Indian Penal Code[39] and Section 3 of the Explosive Substances Act. This was despite the fact that neither of them had sought to take anyone's life. The court relied on the dubious testimonies of prosecution witnesses, who falsely alleged that Bhagat Singh and Batukeshwar Dutt had also fired shots from their guns, thereby justifying a conviction under Section 307. On 12 June 1929, both were sentenced to transportation for life. Following the verdict, Batukeshwar Dutt was sent to the Andaman Islands (Kala Pani), where he spent the next 13 years, while Bhagat Singh was transferred to Lahore, as he was the prime accused in the Lahore Conspiracy Case.

At the time of pronouncing the sentence, Judge Leonard Middleton displayed no leniency, awarding the accused the severest punishment permissible under the applicable provisions. While sentencing Bhagat Singh and Batukeshwar Dutt to life imprisonment, Judge Middleton made the following observation:[40]

> I find it proved that Bhagat Singh threw the first bomb with the intention of causing death or with the intention of causing bodily injury which he knew to be likely to cause death. I find that by doing so he did cause hurt to Sir George Schuster, Mr. P.R. Rao and Mr. Shankar Rao. These facts constitute an offence punishable under

[39]Section 307 of IPC deals with attempt to murder.

[40]National Archives of India, 'File No. Volume II-ACC 306', *Abhilekh-Patal.* Accessed on 7 January 2026.

section 307 I.P.C. with transportation for life or with lesser punishment. I find it proved that Datta threw the second bomb with similar intention and that by doing so he caused hurt to Mr. S.N. Roy and Rai Bahadur A.P. Dube. He too has committed both the offence punishable with transportation for life under Section 307 I.P.C. and the offence similarly punishable under Section 3 of the Explosive Substances Act. I find both the accused guilty of both the offences with which they are charged and convict them accordingly.

[...] The offence is a particularly heinous one and from the retributive point of view merits a severe punishment. The accused have alleged that they hold human life sacred. Their allegation is negatived by their acts. Their attitude throughout has been that their acts are justifiable and justified. With such an attitude their acts are those of men who have not fallen into crime on the spur of the moment but by deliberate design. With such an attitude it is probable that what they have done once they may attempt to do again. From the preventive point of view their offences merit severe punishment. The accused are young men but their acts were deliberate and they had made preparation for those acts of a complicated nature. In these circumstances their youth must not be allowed to lead to the infliction of an inadequate punishment. I sentence Bhagat Singh and B.K. Datta to transportation for life.

Appeal before the Lahore High Court

Bhagat Singh and Batukeshwar Dutt filed Criminal Appeal No. 748 of 1929 before the Lahore High Court, which at that time used to have jurisdiction over Delhi, challenging their conviction under Section 307 of the IPC as awarded by the Sessions Judge. Mr Asaf Ali, who represented the accused, argued that the convictions under Section 307 of the Indian Penal Code could not be legally sustained because there was no intention on the part of the accused to cause the death of any individual. Therefore, they could not be convicted of attempt to murder as defined under Section 307 of the IPC. Unfortunately, their appeal was dismissed on 13 January 1930, despite having strong legal arguments presented in their favour. While delivering the judgment, the Division Bench comprising Justice Cecil Forde and Justice James Addison made the following remarks:[41]

> [...] That Bhagat Singh is a sincere revolutionary I have no doubt, that is to say, he is sincere in the illusion that the word can be improved by destroying the social structure as it now stands and substituting for the rule of law the unrestrained will of the individual. That has always been the defence of the anarchist. But it is no defence to the charges upon which he and his co appellant have been convicted. I am satisfied that both the appellants have been rightly convicted of the offence under S. 307, I.P.C. I am unable to hold that the sentences imposed by the learned Sessions Judge is, under the circumstances, excessive, and I would accordingly dismiss the appeal of both appellants.
>
> Appeal dismissed.

---

[41]Waraich, Malwinderjit S., and Gurdev Singh Sidhu (eds.), *The Hanging of Bhagat Singh: Complete Judgement and Other Documents*, Unistar Publications, Chandigarh, 2005.

The Second Trial: The Lahore Conspiracy Case

Facts of the Case

On 30 October 1928, when the Simon Commission[42] arrived in Lahore, Lala Lajpat Rai led a peaceful and silent protest against it. The police responded with brutal force, severely beating Lajpat Rai with lathis. Eventually, he succumbed to his injuries on 17 November 1928, after sustaining critical wounds in the police lathi charge. Bhagat Singh and his associates sought to avenge the death of Lala Lajpat Rai. Bhagat Singh and Rajguru had originally planned to target the Superintendent of Police, James Scott, who had ordered the lathi charge that led to Rai's fatal injuries. Jai Gopal, another member of the group who later turned approver[43] for the prosecution, was assigned the task of identifying Scott.

However, he mistakenly identified John Saunders as James Scott. On 17 December 1928, at around 4 p.m., Mr Saunders, then serving as Assistant Superintendent of Police, exited the police office, followed by Head Constable Charan Singh. After starting his motorcycle and beginning to ride slowly down the road, Jai Gopal gave a signal. In response, Shivram Rajguru drew his revolver, and moving in Saunders' direction, fired at him as the motorcycle approached. Hit by the bullet, Saunders raised his hands and fell to the ground

---

[42]The Simon Commission was a group of seven members of the British Parliament sent to India under the chairmanship of John Simon. Its purpose was to review the functioning of the Government of India Act, 1919, and recommend constitutional reforms for India. It was a controversial commission as it did not have a single Indian as a member.

[43]An approver is an accomplice in a crime who is granted pardon in exchange for giving a full and truthful testimony against other co-accused persons.

with the motorcycle on top of one leg.

Bhagat Singh then rushed forward and fired several shots from his automatic pistol (Exhibit P. 480) at Saunders as he lay on the ground. Seeing his officer fall, Head Constable Charan Singh gave chase to Bhagat Singh and Rajguru. However, Chandrashekhar Azad was already prepared to deal with any such eventuality. He warned Charan Singh to turn back and not pursue them, but when the head constable ignored the warning, Azad fired at him, killing him on the spot. The trio then made their way into the premises of DAV College, where Azad had arranged bicycles in advance. Mounting the cycles, they rode to a house on Mozang Road in Lahore.

Saunders was later declared dead at the hospital. The police were unable to arrest any of the individuals involved in Saunders' murder for several weeks. It was only after Bhagat Singh was arrested in connection with the Assembly Bomb Case in April 1929 that the authorities discovered Bhagat Singh and his friends' involvement in the Saunders murder.

In the Court of the Lahore
Conspiracy Case Tribunal, Lahore
Constituted under Ordinance No. III of 1930

The initial trial began under charges of conspiracy and waging war against the King-Emperor, under Sections 121, 121A, 122 and 123 of the Indian Penal Code. Later, Section 302 (murder) of the IPC was also added. Eventually, charges were formally framed against the following 15 accused in the Lahore Conspiracy Case:

1. Sukhdev Thapar
2. Kundan Lal
3. Kishori Lal Rattan

4. Des Raj
5. Prem Dutt
6. Bhagat Singh
7. Kanwal Nath Trivedi
8. Jai Dev
9. Shiv Verma
10. Gaya Prasad
11. Mahabir Singh
12. Ajoy Kumar Ghose
13. Jatin Sanyal
14. Bejoy Kumar Sinha
15. Shivaram Rajguru

After some time from the time of framing charges, when the government realized that the trial against Bhagat Singh and the other accused was not progressing, mainly due to the non-cooperation of the accused and the large number of prosecution witnesses (approximately 607), Viceroy Lord Irwin issued Ordinance No. III of 1930. This ordinance established a special tribunal, consisting of three High Court judges of the Lahore High Court, specifically to expedite the trial. Unlike the provisions under the Criminal Procedure Code (CrPC), this ordinance did not allow for any appeal or revision against the tribunal's decisions. Furthermore, it empowered the tribunal to continue the proceedings even in the absence of the accused. In most hearings, the accused resisted being produced before the tribunal, and the trial continued in their absence under Section 9 of the ordinance. On 26 August 1930, after 457 prosecution witnesses had been examined, the prosecution decided to forego the remaining witnesses and closed its case. No defence witnesses appeared for the accused, nor was any list of defence witnesses submitted to be summoned on their behalf.

The case for the prosecution was by and large based on the statements of five approvers, Jai Gopal (PW2), Phonindra Nath Ghose (PW3),[44] Man Mohan Banerji (PW4), Hans Raj Vohra (PW5) and Lalit Kumar Mukerji (PW6).

As there was no direct evidence against Bhagat Singh and other accused, Jai Gopal testified about the involvement of Bhagat Singh and Rajguru in the murder of Saunders, while Hans Raj Vohra provided evidence concerning the activities of the Hindustan Socialist Republican Association (HSRA) and Bhagat Singh's role within it.

The arguments of the prosecutor were concluded on 10 September 1930 and when it was over, the case was adjourned for the judgment till 7 October 1930, as nobody appeared to argue the case on behalf of the accused persons. On 7 October 1930, a special tribunal consisting of Justice G.C. Hilton (President), Justice Abdul Qadir and Justice J.K. Tapp sentenced Bhagat Singh, Sukhdev and Rajguru to death. The five approvers, Jai Gopal, Phonindra Nath Ghose, Man Mohan

---

[44]Phonindra Nath Ghose was once a member of the Hindustán Socialist Republican Association (HSRA), the revolutionary organization to which Bhagat Singh and his comrades belonged. However, during the trial proceedings, Ghose turned approver (state witness) for the British government. His detailed testimony proved crucial for the prosecution in establishing the link between the accused and the conspiracy, significantly strengthening the case against them. His evidence played a key role in securing the conviction and eventual execution of Bhagat Singh, Rajguru, and Sukhdev. However, this act of betrayal did not go unpunished. On 9 November 1932, Phonindra Nath Ghose was assassinated in Bettiah, Bihar, by Baikunth Shukla, a revolutionary from the same region. The killing occurred in the presence of a police constable who had been assigned for Ghose's protection by the British authorities. With this act, the betrayal of Bhagat Singh and HSRA was avenged. Baikunth Shukla was later arrested, and the British government sentenced him to death. He was executed on 14 May 1934, in Gaya Jail.

Banerjee, Hans Raj Vohra[45] and Lalit Kumar Mukherjee, were discharged from custody insofar as any charge against them arising out of the present proceedings was concerned. Following is the list of 15 accused and the punishment given to them by the special tribunal:

Sr. No.	*Accused*	*Sentence*
1	Bhagat Singh	Death sentence
2	Sukhdev Thapar	Death sentence
3	Shivaram Rajguru	Death sentence
4	Kishori Lal Rattan	Transportation for life
5	Des Raj	Acquitted
6	Prem Dutt	Rigorous imprisonment for five years
7	Kanwal Nath Trivedi	Transportation for life
8	Jai Dev	Transportation for life
9	Shiv Verma	Transportation for life
10	Gaya Prasad	Transportation for life
11	Mahabir Singh	Transportation for life
12	Ajoy Kumar Ghosh	Acquitted

[45]Hans Raj Vohra, once a close associate of Sukhdev and an important member of HSRA, turned government approver, the key prosecution witness in the Lahore Conspiracy Case. After being discharged from the trial, he left for England to study at the London School of Economics; his education was sponsored by the British government. Following his studies, and after India's independence, he served as the Washington correspondent for *The Times of India*. Despite his professional success, Vohra lived in obscurity, carrying throughout his life the stigma of being branded a traitor. He avoided public attention, carefully concealing his identity, and never stepping into the limelight. In a letter written to Sukhdev's brother in 1980, he revealed his final wish: 'I hope that by the time I die, I would have been fully forgotten.'

Sr. No.	*Accused*	*Sentence*
13	Jatin Sanyal	Acquitted
14	Bejoy Kumar Sinha	Transportation for life
15	Kundan Lal	Rigorous imprisonment for seven years with solitary confinement

Appeal before the Privy Council

Bhagat Singh was unwilling to file any appeal, as he was prepared to sacrifice his life for the country. He was fully aware of the consequences when he had chosen to throw bombs in the Central Legislative Assembly. He knew that once arrested, the British authorities would not spare him. Therefore, he was neither surprised nor disappointed when he was sentenced to death in the Lahore Conspiracy Case. Ordinarily, a person sentenced to death had the right to file a criminal appeal before the High Court under the CrPC.

However, the British government, fearing the growing influence of Bhagat Singh and his comrades, was determined to carry out the executions swiftly. Viceroy Lord Irwin issued a special ordinance that not only created a special tribunal to try the case but also stripped Bhagat Singh and the others of their right to appeal the tribunal's decision before the High Court. In response, a defence committee was formed with the aim of saving the lives of the accused in the Lahore Conspiracy Case. Since appealing to the Privy Council in Britain was the only legal option left, the committee decided to pursue it. Bhagat Singh, initially reluctant, agreed to file the appeal at the insistence of his father. He consented because he believed that taking the case to the Privy Council would help draw international attention to the cause of freedom of India, especially among the people of Britain.

On 27 February 1931, the judicial committee of the Privy Council comprising five judges, Viscount Dunedin, Lord Thankerton, Lord Russell of Killowen, Sir George Lowndes and Sir Dinshaw Mullah, dismissed this special leave petition of Bhagat Singh and others. D. Pritt, H. Douglas and Sydney Smith had appeared for the petitioners, while A.M. Dunne and W. Wallach had appeared for the Crown. Although counsel for the petitioners raised legal objections before the Privy Council regarding the authority of the Viceroy to promulgate an ordinance, they were unable to persuade the Council to allow the appeal. The following are a list of the objections raised by the counsel for the petitioners:

First: Whether Governor-General could promulgate the ordinance only in the case of emergency or otherwise and whether state of emergency did not exist when he constituted a special tribunal for the trial of Lahore Conspiracy Case?

Second: Whether the constitution of the tribunal pertained to the peace and good governance of British India when the Governor-General could promulgate the ordinance only for peace and good governance?

Viscount Dunedin, delivering the judgment on behalf of all the judges, observed:[46]

> The petitioners ask this Board to find that a state of emergency did not exist. That raises directly the question who is to be the judge of whether a state of

[46]National Archives of India, 'File No. 4/20/31', *Abhilekh-Patal.* Accessed on 7 January 2026.

> emergency exists. A state of emergency is something that does not permit of any exact definition: It connotes a state of matters calling for drastic action which is to be judged as such by someone. It is more than obvious that someone must be the Governor-General and he alone [sic]. Any other view would render utterly inept the whole provision. Emergency demands immediate action, and that action is prescribed to be taken by the Governor-General. It is he alone who can promulgate the ordinance.
>
> It was next said that the ordinance did not conduce to the peace and good government of British India. The same remark applies. The Governor-General is also the judge of that. The power given by S. 72 is an absolute power, without any limits prescribed, except only that it cannot do what the Indian legislature would be unable to do, although it is made clear that it is only to be used in extreme cases of necessity where the good government of India demands it.
>
> [...] Their Lordships must add that, although the Governor-General thought fit to expound the reasons which induced him to promulgate the ordinance, this was not in their Lordships' opinion in any way incumbent on him as a matter of law. Their Lordships, for these reasons, have humbly advised His Majesty that this petition should be dismissed.

On 27 February 1931, when the Privy Council dismissed Bhagat Singh's appeal, from that moment it was only a matter of days before Bhagat Singh, Sukhdev and Rajguru would be executed. 27 February 1931 brought further tragedy for Bhagat Singh and his fellow revolutionaries when Chandrashekhar

Azad, the leader of the military wing of the Hindustan Socialist Republican Association (HSRA), became a martyr. Surrounded by police at Alfred Park in Allahabad, Azad chose to end his life with the final bullet in his pistol rather than surrender and be captured alive.

Last-Minute Efforts to Stall the Execution

After the Privy Council dismissed the special leave petition of Bhagat Singh and his fellow revolutionaries, their lawyers made last-ditch efforts to save their lives. Since the death sentence given by the special tribunal could not be executed on the initially fixed date due to the pendency of the appeal before the Privy Council, the legal team seized this opportunity to file a Habeas Corpus petition under Section 491 of the Criminal Procedure Code before the Lahore High Court.

The petition argued that the special tribunal which had pronounced the death sentence had ceased to exist, and therefore, no competent authority remained to issue a fresh warrant for the execution. According to the law, only the court that pronounced the death sentence had the power to issue the fresh death warrant if the old one could not be executed. However, Justice Bhide of the Lahore High Court dismissed this Habeas Corpus petition, ruling that the local government had the authority to suspend or proceed with the execution, and it was within their discretion to make that decision. The court directed the petitioner to approach the local government under Section 401 of the CrPC. A representation-cum-petition was promptly filed before the local government, but it was rejected without delay. A new date for the execution was then set for 24 March 1931.

On 22 March 1931, just two days before the execution was

scheduled, two more petitions were filed in the Lahore High Court as part of a final attempt to save the lives of Bhagat Singh and his fellow revolutionaries. The first petition argued that the rejection of the representation under Section 401 had created a fresh cause of action. The second petition sought leave to appeal to the Privy Council against Justice Bhide's earlier order dismissing the Habeas Corpus plea.

The Lahore High Court agreed to hear both petitions at 10 a.m. on the morning of 23 March 1931, one day before the execution was scheduled. It was widely understood, including by the government, that if notices were issued in these matters, the execution would have to be postponed. Unfortunately, the court dismissed both petitions on the same day, and within a few hours, the government proceeded to carry out the death sentences of Bhagat Singh, Rajguru and Sukhdev.

Aftermath

Bhagat Singh, Sukhdev and Rajguru were executed in haste on 23 March 1931 in Lahore Jail, nearly twelve hours before the scheduled time. The execution itself was highly unusual. As per the jail manual, death sentences were to be carried out in the morning, but fearing public outrage, the British advanced the hanging to the evening, a day earlier than planned. At the time of their martyrdom, Bhagat Singh and Sukhdev Thapar were just 24 years old, while Rajguru was only 23. When Bhagat Singh volunteered to throw bombs in the Central Legislative Assembly, Chandrashekhar Azad knew that Bhagat Singh's days were limited. He told his fellow revolutionary, Shiv Verma, 'In a few days, history will claim them (Bhagat Singh and Batukeshwar Dutt), and only the legend will survive through the corridors of time.'

Countless men and women have laid down their lives for India's freedom, many fading into obscurity, remembered by none. Only a few survive in the nation's collective memory, and among them, Bhagat Singh, Sukhdev, and Rajguru stand immortal, honoured for embracing death at such a young age. Bhagat Singh's popularity, in a remarkably short span, rose to the level of Mahatma Gandhi's.

The way the trial and execution of Bhagat Singh was conducted shattered the British claim of upholding equality and justice within the Empire. The promulgation of the Ordinance by Lord Irwin, which circumvented the regular legal process and denied them the right to appeal before the High Court, demonstrated how the colonial government could twist the law to silence the voices of freedom fighters. Bhagat Singh may have died, but his memory continues to live on in the hearts of millions.

SIX

TRIAL OF RAM PRASAD BISMIL AND ASHFAQULLA KHAN (KAKORI CONSPIRACY CASE)

On 9 August 1925, at around 6.30 p.m., the Moradabad–Lucknow Express departed from Kakori railway station and was heading toward Alamnagar when a few miles from Kakori, it came to an abrupt halt. Among the passengers of this train was Ahmad Ali, a young legal practitioner, who was travelling separately from his wife, who was in the women's compartment. When the train suddenly stopped, Ahmad Ali got down and began walking toward his wife's compartment to check on her well-being.

As he proceeded, he noticed four to five men standing near the second-class compartment but paid no attention to them and continued walking. Among these men was Manmath Nath Gupta. Gupta, along with his friends, was in the process of executing a plan to loot government money which was being transported on this train. Gupta warned Ahmad Ali to return to his compartment, but Ahmad Ali ignored his warning and continued walking towards his wife's carriage. In a moment of panic, the already anxious Gupta fired a shot at Ahmad Ali, who died instantly. Ahmad Ali was the only unfortunate victim of the famous Kakori Train Robbery.

Years later, in 1997, in a Doordarshan interview for the series 'Sarfaroshi ki Tamanna', an ageing Manmath Nath Gupta, recounted remorsefully, in his trembling voice, the fateful error that had haunted him for life. 'I had no intention to kill,' he confessed. 'But I did.' And because of that single tragic mistake, Ram Prasad Bismil and Ashfaqulla Khan, his dearest colleagues in the Hindustan Republican Association (HRA), were sent to the gallows.

This sensational train robbery, which is known as Kakori Train Robbery in the history of the Indian freedom struggle, shocked the British government to its core. The revolutionaries first threw the iron chest, containing government funds collected from various railway stations, out of the train's brake van. They then broke it open, seized the cash and disappeared. This daring act and the dramatic escape of the looters without leaving any trace of any kind was an object of astonishment both to the government and to the public.[47] The daring individuals who executed this sensational act of robbery—Ram Prasad Bismil, Ashfaqulla Khan, Chandrashekhar Azad, Manmath Nath Gupta, and others—were members of the HRA.

Hindustan Republican Association

The Hindustan Republican Association was founded in 1924 by Sachindra Nath Sanyal[48] with the aim of establishing a democratic and republican India. Its prominent members, such as Ram Prasad Bismil, Ashfaqulla Khan, Chandrashekhar Azad

---

[47]Chatterjee, Jogesh Chandra, *In Search of Freedom*, Paresh Chandra Chatterjee, Calcutta, 1967.

[48]Chapter nine will deal with his story in greater detail.

and Jogesh Chandra Chatterjee, used to believe that India's independence would not be achieved through constitutional means alone and it required an armed revolution.

The members of HRA knew that to sustain this revolutionary struggle, funds were essential; therefore it resolved to raise funds by targeting government resources, particularly through robberies, and when government funds were not accessible, then under the direction of Ram Prasad Bismil, several robberies were carried out targeting individuals known for their loyalty to the British. The Kakori Train Robbery was executed with a similar objective—seizing government money to fund the movement. The killing of Mr Ahmad Ali, however, was never part of the plan; it occurred in the heat of the moment, an unintended tragedy amidst the chaos.

Investigation

The Kakori Train Robbery sent shockwaves through the British government, placing immense pressure on the colonial administration to swiftly apprehend those responsible. Therefore, the investigation was handed over to Mr R.A. Horton, Superintendent of Police of Criminal Investigation Department (CID). R.A. Horton began focusing his investigation on political suspects. A breakthrough in the investigation came when some of the currency notes looted during the Kakori Train Robbery were traced to Shahjahanpur, where Ram Prasad Bismil was residing at the time. Horton learnt from his sources that Indu Bhushan Mitra, a student (who would later turn approver), was acting as a postal intermediary for Bismil, receiving letters on his behalf. Horton approached the headmaster of Mitra's school and instructed him to copy the content of any incoming letters. Through this method, the CID was able to intercept crucial information, including the details of an upcoming meeting of the HRA's provincial council, scheduled to take place at the Vaishya Orphanage in Meerut on 13 and 14 September 1925. The police secretly monitored this gathering, and beginning on 26 September, launched a province-wide operation of arrests and searches targeting those who had attended or were associated with the HRA. Nearly forty-three individuals including Ram Prasad Bismil were arrested across the region. Indu Bhushan Mitra and Banarsi Lal (a former HRA member) turned approvers, providing significant intelligence about the location of arms, ammunition and other seditious materials. Some of the accused like Sachindra Nath Sanyal and Rajendra Nath Lahiri were brought from Calcutta, where they were already serving sentences in connection with the Dakshineswar Bomb Case. Meanwhile, Sachindra Nath Bakshi, Ashfaqulla Khan and Chandrashekhar Azad went underground to evade arrest.

THE TRIAL

King-Emperor v. Benoari Lal[49] *& Ors.*
Session Trial No. 1 of 1926

Judge: A. Hamilton (I.C.S.) Special Session Judge, Lucknow Court

Following the CID investigation, 43 individuals were arrested in connection with the case. However, only 21 of them, including Ram Prasad Bismil, Roshan Singh and Rajendra Nath Lahiri, were ultimately produced before the Magistrate

[49]Benoari Lal refers to Banwari Lal, the historical figure. This spelling has been used in legal documentation.

as formal accused. The trial commenced on 4 January 1926 before the Court of the Special Magistrate, Syed Ainuddin (who was widely perceived as being overly biased against the revolutionaries). The Magistrate, as expected, soon proved to be more hostile towards the revolutionaries than even the British authorities themselves. He went so far as to provide false testimony under oath before the Special Sessions Judge.

In clear violation of the principles of a fair criminal trial, he participated in the identification parade, acted as the committal magistrate, and later deposed before the Sessions Court, a role that should have been kept separate to ensure impartiality. Yet, there was no authority willing to hear the revolutionaries' pleas, particularly when the entire colonial machinery seemed determined to secure their execution by any means necessary.

Moreover, the British government had deliberately chosen Muslim magistrates or Muslim officials to deal with revolutionaries, as there was a general feeling that the revolutionary movement was mainly a Hindu movement and Muslims should not therefore make common cause with the accused.[50] Banarsi Lal, who had turned approver, was the first witness examined by the prosecution, led by advocate Pandit Jagat Narain Mullah. The defence team, as a matter of strategy, chose not to cross-examine witnesses during the magistrate's court proceedings. Consequently, only the prosecution's evidence was recorded at that stage, while the defence counsel merely observed. In total, 247 witnesses were presented by the prosecution.

---

[50]Chatterji, Jogesh Chandra, *In Search of Freedom*, Paresh Chandra Chatterjee, Calcutta, 1967.

Charges against the Accused

The following charges were formally brought against all the 21 accused.

First Charge: During the years 1924 and 1925, at different places in Uttar Pradesh, the accused had conspired with one another to deprive the King-Emperor of the sovereignty of British India and thereby committed an offence punishable under Section 121A[51] of IPC.

Second Charge: In pursuance of the aims of the aforesaid conspiracy and in order to collect funds (for seditious and revolutionary propaganda and for purchase of arms and ammunition, etc.), the accused did agree with one another to commit the following armed dacoities with murder as a result (under Sections 120B and 396[52] of IPC):

- (i) Bamruali Dacoity at the house of Baldeo Prasad on 25.12.1924
- (ii) Bichpuri Dacoity at the house of Toti Kurmi on 09.03.1925
- (iii) Dwarkapur Dacoity at the house of Sheo Ratan Bania on 24.05.1925
- (iv) Train Dacoity on the 8 down train between Kakori and Alamnagar stations on 09.08.1925

The prosecution's case rested almost entirely on the testimonies of the three approvers: Banarsi Lal, Indu Bhushan Mitra and

[51]Section 121A of the IPC deals with conspiracy to commit offences like waging or attempting to wage, or abetting the waging of, war against the King-Emperor (Government of India, now).

[52]Section 396 of the IPC deals with dacoity with murder.

Banwari Lal. Among them, Banarsi Lal, the principal approver, was unable to provide substantial evidence directly linking the accused to the Kakori Train Robbery. It was Banwari Lal's testimony that proved most damaging to Ram Prasad Bismil, Ashfaqulla Khan and Rajendra Nath Lahiri. Having personally participated in the Kakori operation, Banwari Lal served as the first account witness, offering a direct narrative of the incident.

In addition to the oral testimonies, the prosecution relied heavily on three key documents:

(1) The Constitution of the Hindustan Republican Association
(2) A pamphlet titled 'Revolutionary', circulated on behalf of the Association
(3) The recorded proceedings of the HRA's council meeting

In an interesting turn of events, Pandit Motilal Nehru, then a member of the Central Legislative Assembly, travelled to Lucknow to arrange legal representation for the accused revolutionaries. He initially approached Pandit Jagat Narayan Mullah, a prominent criminal lawyer of the city, who agreed to take up the defence but on one condition: he would dedicate 20 days each month to the case, reserving the remaining 10 days for his private practice. Motilal Nehru, however, found this unacceptable and, disappointed by Mullah's stance, declined the offer. Instead, he established a Defence Committee under the leadership of Pandit Govind Ballabh Pant. Esteemed lawyers like Pandit Govind Ballabh Pant, Mohanlal Saxena, Pandit Harkaran Nath Mishra and C.B. Gupta joined the committee and went on to represent most of the accused before the Sessions Court. To Pandit Motilal Nehru's dismay, however, Jagat Narayan Mullah later accepted the CID's offer to lead the prosecution and appeared throughout the trial on behalf of the Crown/Prosecution.[53]

The trial of the Kakori Conspiracy Case drew widespread attention from both the public and the press. Indian newspapers closely followed every detail, documenting courtroom developments and the actions of the accused. For revolutionaries like Ram Prasad Bismil, the courtroom became an unexpected platform, a rare opportunity to voice their convictions and thoughts to the nation. Each day, when Bismil and his fellow revolutionaries stepped out of the police van and entered the courtroom premises, they would sing loudly from Bismil Azimabadi's iconic poem, '*Sarfaroshi ki tamanna ab hamare dil mein hai*'. And every time the judge entered the courtroom, all the accused would rise and greet him in unison with a thunderous chant of '*Vande Mataram*'.

The courtroom was packed on every hearing date with curious citizens, impassioned supporters and eager journalists documenting the unfolding trial. On one such day, Bismil and the others were taken by surprise when they spotted a young man sitting quietly among the crowd: Sardar Bhagat Singh. A fellow revolutionary and member of the HRA, Bhagat Singh had slipped in unnoticed to observe the proceedings. Dressed sharply and maintaining his trademark calm smile, he sat silently the entire day. Although the courtroom was swarming with policemen and CID officers, no one recognized the dignified Sikh youth in their midst. It was an act of audacity, attending the trial under such surveillance, yet it spoke volumes

---

[53]Waraich, Malwinderjit, *Hanging of Ram Prasad Bismil*, Unistar, Chandigarh, 2007.

of the courage and solidarity that bound these revolutionaries together.

Judgment Day

On the day of the verdict, i.e. 6 April 1927, the revolutionaries sat silently inside the police vehicle, their expressions solemn and subdued. Sensing the heavy mood, Ram Prasad Bismil attempted to lift their spirits. He began to sing, 'Sarfaroshi ki tamanna ab hamare dil mein hai.' As they stepped out of the vehicle and walked into the courtroom, his fellow revolutionaries joined in, their collective voices echoing through the corridors of court. As the judge entered, the courtroom once again resonated with the united cry of 'Vande Mataram', offered by the revolutionaries as a mark of defiance and dignity.

Without delay, Judge A. Hamilton of the Special Sessions Court, Lucknow, delivered his judgment in the Kakori Conspiracy Case. He sentenced Ram Prasad Bismil, Rajendra Nath Lahiri and Thakur Roshan Singh to death. While the capital punishment for Bismil and Lahiri had been somewhat anticipated, the inclusion of Thakur Roshan Singh came as a shock as it was unexpected even by those who were closely following the trial. Judge Hamilton was so visibly uneasy while pronouncing the verdict that immediately after delivering it, he boarded a train to Bombay, and from there, took a ship to London. After that he never returned to India. Perhaps the weight of his guilt and moral uncertainty drove him away from the very land where he had passed the fateful sentence.

Of the 21 accused, Indu Bhushan Mitra and Banarsi Lal (the principal approvers) were discharged from the trial by the court after they turned government witnesses and aided the prosecution in securing convictions against the other revolutionaries. Banwari Lal, another approver who had directly participated in the Kakori Train Robbery, was not fully discharged but was granted leniency and sentenced to five years' imprisonment. True to his name, Chandrashekhar Azad remained untraceable and successfully evaded arrest. Judge A. Hamilton ultimately convicted 17 revolutionaries, sentencing them as follows:

Sr. No.	*Accused*	*Sections*	*Sentence*
1	Banwari Lal	121A/120B/396	5 years of rigorous imprisonment
2	Bhupendra Nath Sanyal	121A/120B/396	5 years of rigorous imprisonment
3	Govind Charan Kar	121A/120B/396	10 years of rigorous imprisonment
4	Jogesh Chandar Chatterji	121A/120B/396	10 years of rigorous imprisonment
5	Makundi Lal	121A/120B/396	10 years of rigorous imprisonment
6	Manmath Nath Gupta	121A/120B/396	14 years of rigorous imprisonment
7	Parnawesh Kumar Chatterji	121A/120B/396	5 years of rigorous imprisonment
8	Prem Kishan Khanna	121A/120B/396	5 years of rigorous imprisonment
9	Rajendra Nath Lahiri	121A/120B/396	Death sentence

Sr. No.	*Accused*	*Sections*	*Sentence*
10	Raj Kumar Sinha	121A/120B/396	5 years of rigorous imprisonment
11	Ram Dulare Trivedi	121A/120B/396	5 years of rigorous imprisonment
12	Ram Kishan Khattri	121A/120B/396	10 years of rigorous imprisonment
13	Ram Nath Pande	121A/120B/396	5 years of rigorous imprisonment
14	Ram Prasad Bismil	121A/120B/396	Death sentence
15	Raushan Singh	121A/120B/396	Death sentence
16	Sachindra Nath Sanyal	121A/120B/396	Life imprisonment
17	Vishnu Saran Dublis	121A/120B/396	7 years of rigorous imprisonment

Ashfaqulla Khan

Ashfaqulla Khan was a Pathan from Shahjahanpur and an active member of the HRA. Initially Ram Prasad Bismil did not want Ashfaqulla Khan to join the revolutionaries but Ashfaq's earnest devotion changed his attitude and soon he became Ram Prasad's most trusted lieutenant.[54]

Ashfaqulla Khan was also one of the main accused in the Kakori Train Robbery. Initially, he could not be arrested and was on the run. But eventually he was arrested in Delhi after

[54]Chatterji, Jogesh Chandra, *In Search of Freedom*, Paresh Chandra Chatterjee, Calcutta, 1958.

one of his close associates betrayed him, leaking details of his whereabouts to the police. Syed Ainuddin, who was the Committing Magistrate, was sent to Delhi where Ashfaqulla was arrested. Then he escorted him from Delhi to Lucknow by train. His object was to pursue him as a fellow Muslim and extract information about the other revolutionaries But Ashfaqulla Khan did not budge and did not fall in his trap. His trial was presided over by Judge J.R.W. Bennett, Special Sessions Judge, Lucknow. However, the proceedings were widely perceived as a mere formality, a farce, given that Judge A. Hamilton had already handed down death sentences to Ashfaqulla's friends in HRA on identical charges. On 13 July 1927, the court delivered its verdict. As anticipated, Ashfaqulla Khan was convicted under Sections 121A, 120B and 396 of the Indian Penal Code, and handed the death penalty. Ashfaqulla Khan was the only Muslim revolutionary who was hanged on the charge of conspiracy to deprive the King-Emperor of his sovereignty over British India.

Short Introductions of Some of the Main Accused in the Kakori Conspiracy Case

1. **Ram Prasad Bismil:** He was the provincial organizer of the HRA. Ashfaqulla Khan was appointed as his assistant. Ram Prasad had a literary taste and used to write articles and poems.[55] Besides Hindi, he also knew other languages like Urdu, English and Bengali. He was only 29 years old at the time of the verdict.
2. **Roshan Singh:** Roshan Singh was born in a village in Shahjahanpur. Though not highly educated, he was

---

[55]Ibid.

known for his intelligence and practical wisdom. While imprisoned in Lucknow jail, he undertook a 16-day hunger strike demanding better treatment for political prisoners like himself. Unlike Ram Prasad Bismil and Ashfaqulla Khan, Roshan Singh was not sentenced to death in the Kakori Train Robbery case; instead, he was awarded five years of rigorous imprisonment. However, he was later given the death penalty in connection with another dacoity case carried out by him and his revolutionary friends. Despite repeated pleas from family and friends, he refused to sign any mercy petition. In Lucknow Jail, a peepal tree still stands as a symbol of his courage. Planted by Roshan Singh himself, the tree is said to convey his belief that while he might not live to see it grow, its shade would someday offer solace to future generations. The tree, located just behind his prison barrack, remains a living memorial to a man who gave everything for his country's future.

3. **Rajendra Nath Lahiri:** Rajendra Nath Lahiri had travelled to Calcutta where he learned the art of bomb-making under the guidance of the HRA. A prominent leader in the Kakori Conspiracy Case, after Kakori he returned to Calcutta, where he was arrested in connection with the Dakshineswar Bomb Case and sentenced to 10 years of imprisonment. Subsequently, he was brought to Lucknow to face trial for his role in the Kakori Conspiracy Case and was ultimately awarded the death penalty. An academic as well as a revolutionary, Lahiri served as the Honorary Secretary of the Bengal Sahitya Parishad at Banaras Hindu University (BHU). He held both BA and MA degrees in History.
4. **Sachindra Nath Sanyal:** In his early youth, Sachindra Nath Sanyal, along with his associates, established the

Anushilan Samiti in Banaras in 1909. A close companion of Rash Bihari Bose, Sanyal played a pivotal role in the revolutionary movement. In the Banaras Conspiracy Case, he was sentenced to transportation for life and deported to the Cellular Jail in the Andaman Islands. He was released in 1920 under a royal amnesty but soon resumed his revolutionary activities, first in Uttar Pradesh and later in Bengal, under the banner of the HRA, an organization he himself had founded. Sanyal was later implicated in the Kakori Conspiracy Case as well, sentenced to life imprisonment once again and sent back to the Andamans. He holds the rare and sombre distinction of being the first Indian revolutionary to receive the Kala Pani sentence twice in his lifetime.

5. **Manmath Nath Gupta:** Manmath Nath Gupta was from Banaras and was a student at Kashi Vidyapith. He was the youngest among the accused in the Kakori Conspiracy Case. In consideration of his young age, the court sentenced him to 14 years of imprisonment.

APPEAL BEFORE CHIEF COURT OF OUDH

(Now known as Allahabad High Court)

Ram Prasad Bismil & Ors. v. King-Emperor

Criminal Appeal No. 186/187/189 of 1927

On the advice of their legal team, Ram Prasad, Rajendra Nath Lahiri and Roshan Singh appealed against their convictions and sentences. Sachindra Nath Sanyal did not appeal. Ashfaqulla Khan also filed an appeal. While dismissing their Appeal on 22 August 1927 and confirming the death sentences, the Appellate Court which comprised Chief Justice

Louis Stuart and Justice Muhammad Raza held that:

> We find that it is proved overwhelmingly that a conspiracy came into being in the United provinces in July 1924 to deprive the king emperor of the sovereignty of British India, and that the persons who were controlling the conspiracy as the inner circle further conspired to commit dacoities in which fire-arms were intended to be used, in order to obtain funds with which to purchase arms and ammunition and to carry on revolutionary propaganda. We find that the evidence clearly shows that those persons contemplated that fire-arms should be used in order to enable the dacoities to be committed effectively and with impunity, that they foresaw and realized that murder was a probable and likely consequence of those dacoities and that thus it is established that there was within the conspiracy to deprive the king-emperor of the sovereignty of British India a conspiracy to commit dacoities with murder.

Aftermath

Ram Prasad Bismil was not just a revolutionary in action, but a poet at heart. Renowned for his stirring verses and powerful prose, he emerged as a rare blend of patriot and poet. An ideologue who fought with both the sword and the pen, his writings and poems, composed under the pen names 'Bismil', 'Ram' and 'Agyat', are still sung as a symbol of protest in modern times. Bismil's thoughts and writing shattered the myth that revolutionaries were merely impulsive or reckless youths.

When Bismil realized that death was inevitable, he began

writing his autobiography, *Atamkatha*, in jail. Driven by the belief that future generations must know the ideals for which he lived and died, he swiftly smuggled his manuscript out of jail. It was as if he foresaw that their sacrifices would be forgotten and this was his way of inscribing himself into the soul of a nation yet to awaken.

On 17 December 1927, a day before his execution in Gorakhpur Jail, Ram Prasad Bismil was visited by his mother. The moment he saw his mother, tears started rolling down the eyes of Ram Prasad Bismil. Witnessing this, Bismil's mother said:[56]

> 'I have been under the impression that my son is brave, on hearing of whose name, even the British Government trembles. I had never thought he was scared of death. If you were to die weeping, why on earth did you take this path'[.] Moved by her words, Bismil gently assured her that his tears were not out of fear, but a reflection of his deep love and affection for her.

Bhagat Singh and other members of HRA made repeated efforts to rescue Bismil from jail, devising detailed plans to secure his release. However, each attempt failed for one reason or another. On one occasion, after failing to free Bismil due to heightened security, Bhagat Singh returned to his room and wept bitterly. In his book *In Search of Freedom*, Jogesh Chandra Chatterji recounts that when they realized the court was determined to impose the maximum punishment on the accused and that there was no hope of justice from

---

[56]Waraich, Malwinderjit, *Hanging of Ram Prasad Bismil*, Unistar, Chandigarh, 2007.

the British court, they decided, on the directive of the HRA, to escape from jail. However, the plan ultimately failed. He narrates their daring jail-break attempt in the following words:

> Hacksaw blades were smuggled inside and gratings of the windows of Bismil were cut unnoticed. Bismil, myself, G. G. Kar and M. N. Gupta—These four were to escape. We were to scale the inside row of walls and go near the drain of the main wall and push through a stick, the other end of which would be fastened with a string which again would be held by our friends outside. As soon as we pushed the stick the friends would know of our arrival and would throw a rope ladder over the wall for us and catch hold of the other end and thus, we would scale the wall one by one.
>
> We administered sleeping drugs to one of the two warders on duty outside and also to the two convict watchmen inside our barrack. The warder outside was fast-asleep under the influence of the drug, but the second warden was very alert. The drug did not have much effect on one of the convict watchmen also. He was feeling sleepy but was struggling to keep himself awake, particularly because the warder outside was again and again shouting to keep him alert. Because of this we could not get out.
>
> Outside the main wall our friends, were waiting with the rope ladder, arms and even bombs. When they came to the spot, they found an armed warder was patrolling covering that part of the wall only which was over-looking our barrack. When they saw this, they themselves formed into two groups, one for over-powering the

> armed warder and the other to help us to get out by throwing the rope ladder for us and then to see that we could jump down smoothly. They remained there the whole night and went away disappointed owing to our failure to get out of our barracks.

The British government somehow got wind of the jail-break plan of the accused and immediately after the confirmation of their sentences, all four condemned revolutionaries were transferred to separate jails: Gorakhpur, Faizabad, Allahabad and Gonda. There they were executed individually. Rajendra Nath Lahiri was the first to be sent to the gallows, hanged on 17 December 1927 in Gonda Jail. On 19 December 1927, Ram Prasad Bismil was executed in Gorakhpur Jail, Ashfaqulla Khan in Faizabad Jail and Roshan Singh in Allahabad Jail.

SEVEN

TRIALS OF VINAYAK DAMODAR SAVARKAR (NASIK CONSPIRACY CASE)

Vinayak Damodar Savarkar was a law student residing at India House in London, when he was deported to India to face trial in the famous Nasik Conspiracy Case. The case arose from the assassination of District Collector A.M. Jackson, who was shot dead in a theatre in Nasik by a young revolutionary named Anant Laxman Kanhere. The British authorities suspected that the pistol used in the assassination of Mr Jackson had been supplied by Savarkar from London. They further believed that those involved in the murder were either directly connected with Savarkar or ideologically influenced by him and his revolutionary organization, Abhinav Bharat Society. Hence, British Indian authorities quickly coordinated with the London Police to secure Savarkar's arrest. Fully aware that he was being targeted unjustly and disillusioned with any hope of a fair trial under British law in India, Savarkar attempted a daring escape. While being transported to India by sea, he tried to escape from the ship when it docked at Marseille, France, in a desperate bid for freedom.

However, he was soon recaptured, this time heavily chained

until the ship reached India. What followed was a complex legal battle. The British government, fearing Savarkar's influence in India, set up a special tribunal composed of Bombay High Court judges to ensure a swift and conclusive trial. To prolong his detention, Savarkar was implicated in not one but two separate criminal trials, both aimed at securing the harshest possible punishment. As anticipated, Savarkar was found guilty in both cases and sentenced to transportation for life twice. He was sent to the notorious Cellular Jail in the Andaman Islands, a prison designed for the most dangerous criminals and political prisoners. Since each sentence of transportation for life amounted to 25 years, Savarkar was effectively facing 50 years in solitary confinement. However, before delving into the details of the Savarkar trial, it is essential to understand the trial faced by Anant Laxman Kanhere and six others who were convicted for the assassination of District Collector A.M. Jackson.

NASIK CONSPIRACY CASE

In the High Court of Judicature at Bombay
King-Emperor v. Anant Laxman Kanhere & Ors.
Special Bench Case No. 1 of 1910

As early as 1908, a group of young men in Nasik formed a secret society with the aim of securing India's independence through revolutionary means. Membership in the society required the mandatory taking of an oath of secrecy. The organization's primary objective was to achieve freedom through armed struggle. To further this cause, its members began collecting weapons, manufacturing explosives and administering the oath to a growing number of young men not only in Nasik but other surrounding districts as well. The original members of this secret society were K.G. Karve, V.N. Deshpande and S.R. Soman. Subsequently they were joined by G.V. Vaidya, who later became the keeper of the weapons of the society.

Sometime in June 1909, Vaidya visited Aurangabad, where he met Anant Laxman Kanhere for the first time through a common friend. Anant learned from Vaidya of the secret society and expressed his willingness to join the society, and suggested that something big should be done in order to draw the attention of people towards their goal. On the request of Anant, in the middle of September 1909, Vaidya sent him to Nasik to meet other members of the society and it was there that Anant became acquainted with V.N. Deshpande, S.R. Soman and W.N. Joshi. It was during this meeting that the proposal to assassinate Mr Jackson, the District Collector of Nasik, was discussed and the responsibility for carrying out this task was entrusted to Anant Laxman Kanhere.

A.M. Jackson was also known as Pandit Jackson among the general public because of his deep knowledge of Hindi, Sanskrit and the Hindu religion. He was not only the District Collector of Nasik but also a learned Indologist and historian. Yet, Mr Jackson became the target of the Society because not only did he have knowledge of the Society's activities but it was also under his direction that Ganesh Damodar Savarkar (elder brother of Vinayak Damodar Savarkar) was arrested for writing *Laghu Abhinav Bharat*[57] and eventually sent to Andaman to serve his imprisonment.

---

[57]*Laghu Abhinav Bharat* was a book brought out by Abhinav Bharat Society, a revolutionary organization founded by Vinayak Damodar Savarkar. The book contained provocative content intended to inspire and mobilize individuals to join the revolutionary movement.

Once the proposal was unanimously agreed upon, Anant visited the Collector's office at least twice, accompanied by his friends, to clearly identify Mr Jackson and to ensure that there should be no mistake in identifying him at the time of executing their plan. On most of these occasions, he was accompanied by Waman Joshi. G.V. Vaidya supplied Anant with the pistol for the task. The other accused, V.N. Deshpande, S.R. Soman and W.N. Joshi, took Anant to a secluded location where they trained him to use the pistol provided by Vaidya. During his stay in Nasik, Anant was also taken to a photographer by Waman Joshi to have his photograph taken. Although K.G. Karve, who was the recognized head of the Society, was not in the initial meeting, he later gave his assent to the proposal to assassinate Mr Jackson.

While preparations to assassinate Mr Jackson were underway, in December 1909, Anant and other members of the Society received information that Mr Jackson had been transferred to Bombay and would soon be leaving Nasik. In response, the group unanimously agreed to carry out the plan before his departure. When they later learned that Mr Jackson would be watching a Marathi play by the name of 'Sangeet Sharada' in Vijayanand Theatre, Nasik, a performance to be organized in his honour on 21 December 1909, they decided that this occasion would provide the ideal opportunity for carrying out the assassination.

Before Anant proceeded to the theatre, S.R. Soman handed him a packet of poison to use in case he was captured and unable to shoot himself. K.G. Karve gave him a letter titled 'Murder for Murder'. Subsequently, Karve made his way to the theatre from his own residence, carrying a small pistol in case any unforeseen situation arose. Meanwhile, V.N. Deshpande escorted Anant to the theatre, left him near the entrance and then joined Karve at a different section of the venue.

At around 9.30 p.m., Mr Jackson arrived at the theatre. As he made his way to his seat, 18-year-old Anant Laxman Kanhere pulled out his pistol and shot him at close range. Following the assassination, Anant attempted to shoot himself but was quickly overpowered and captured by those present at the scene. The assassination of a District Collector sent shockwaves through the British administration. In response, the authorities acted swiftly and arrested many individuals who were connected with this secret society directly or indirectly.

Out of several individuals arrested, the following seven accused were committed to trial on charges related to the murder of Mr Jackson:

(i) Anant Laxman Kanhere
(ii) Krishnaji Gopal Karve
(iii) Vinayak Narayan Deshpande
(iv) Shankar Ramchandra Soman
(v) Waman Narayan Joshi
(vi) Ganesh Balaji Vaidya
(vii) Dattatraya Pandurang Joshi

Out of these seven accused who were committed to the special court, Anant Laxman Kanhere was charged with murder under Section 302,[58] and the others were charged with aiding and facilitating the murder. Kanhere pleaded guilty before the court and accepted that he had murdered Mr Jackson but claimed that he had no companions. But still the trial court proceeded

[58]Section 302 of the Indian Penal Code (IPC) deals with punishment for murder.

against the other accused. To conduct the trial against Kanhere and the six other accused, the British government had invoked Section 11[59] of the Indian Criminal Law Amendment Act, 1908, and constituted a special court comprising Bombay High Court judges to try the case.

According to the prosecution, there was ample evidence against the accused persons. The larger Browning pistol, the revolver, the paper headed 'Murder for Murder', and the packet of poison had been seized from Kanhere when he was arrested. Hence, on the basis of evidence gathered by the police, the Special Court had concluded that Karve, Deshpande and Soman were aware of the intention to kill Mr Jackson that night, and each one of them had taken an active part in the preparations immediately before the assassination. The court also observed that two of the three accused, i.e., Karve, and Deshpande, were present at the assassination site and were guiding Anant in his task.

On 29 March 1910, within a span of three months, the special court concluded the trial and found all seven accused guilty, sentencing them according to their respective roles in the crime. The principal accused, Anant Laxman Kanhere, was awarded the death penalty. K.G. Karve and V.N. Deshpande were also sentenced to death, as they had actively participated in the conspiracy to assassinate and were present at the scene during Mr Jackson's assassination. S.R. Soman, W.N. Joshi and G.B. Vaidya were sentenced to transportation for life, while D.P. Joshi received two years of rigorous imprisonment.

---

[59]This provision allows the government to refer certain offences such as conspiracies and political assassinations to special courts with simplified procedures. It also placed restrictions on the right to appeal, thereby making it more difficult for convictions to be overturned.

The First Trial of Vinayak Damodar Savarkar

During the investigation into the assassination of District Magistrate A.M.T. Jackson, the police soon uncovered the existence of a clandestine network of young revolutionaries. An underground association or society was found to be actively engaged in revolutionary activities across several cities in the Deccan region including Nasik, Pune, Bombay, Pen, Poona, Yeola and Aurangabad. At the heart of this secret association were Vinayak Damodar Savarkar and his elder brother, Ganesh Savarkar, who led this association under the name of 'Abhinav Bharat'. The association's core objective was to secure India's independence through direct action, which included political assassinations and the use of firearms and explosives.

Savarkar's secret society, however, was not alone in its vision. By the last decade of the 19th century, numerous such groups had sprung up in the Deccan, particularly among students. These societies were often centred around gymnasiums for physical training and were involved in public celebration of festivals like Ganesh Utsav where rousing patriotic songs would be sung and legendary figures like Chhatrapati Shivaji commemorated. These were intended to instil a martial spirit and pride in India's heritage.

One such society founded by Vinayak and Ganesh Savarkar before 1906 was Mitra Mela, a group composed primarily of young Brahmin men. Mitra Mela became a vibrant centre for revolutionary thought. Regular meetings were held at Ganesh Savarkar's residence, where the young men read and re-read the biographies of revolutionary figures like Giuseppe Mazzini, Shivaji Maharaj and Sant Ramdas. These sessions were not just for engaging in patriotic discussions but were the active planning grounds where strategies for attaining India's independence were debated.

Although the methods promoted by Mitra Mela included public education through speeches, books and patriotic songs, covert preparations for an armed uprising such as the procurement and stockpiling of weapons and explosives was also very much a part of its activities. This cultural awakening soon transformed to a revolutionary storm and became very popular in Deccan. Vinayak Savarkar was one of the most active, and probably the most stimulating, members of the Mitra Mela. He had been actively delivering fiery speeches in Poona and Nasik, aimed at igniting a spirit of nationalism and stirring deep resentment against British colonial rule. His talks emphasized the importance of mental discipline and physical training as essential tools to prepare the youth for a future uprising in the fight for India's independence.

But in mid-June 1906, Vinayak Damodar Savarkar was awarded a scholarship by Shyamji Krishna Varma, the founder of India House in England. With this support, Savarkar decided to pursue legal studies in England. Before the departure of Vinayak Savarkar for England, the Mitra Mela had developed into or given birth to Abhinav Bharat or Young India Society, a title which was borrowed from the Young Italy[60] of Mazzini. Its objectives were unquestionably revolutionary. The aim of its members was to be prepared for war. The Abhinav Bharat Society used to operate with such secrecy that its existence remained undiscovered by the authorities until the assassination of Mr Jackson on 21 December 1909.

[60]Young Italy was an Italian political movement founded in 1831 by Giuseppe Mazzini.

As discussed earlier, one of the key reasons behind Mr Jackson's assassination was the role he played as the District Magistrate of Nasik, during which he became aware of the activities of Abhinav Bharat and began monitoring them closely. Upon discovering more about the organization, he ordered the arrest of Ganesh Savarkar for authoring a book titled *Laghu Abhinav Bharatmala*, which he considered seditious. The provocative content of the book ultimately led to Ganesh Savarkar's conviction and deportation to the Andaman Islands. This act deeply enraged the revolutionaries operating covertly in the Deccan, many of whom were inspired by the ideals of Abhinav Bharat.

Activities of V.D. Savarkar in England

When Vinayak Savarkar arrived in England in 1906, he chose to reside at India House in London, which had by then become a prominent centre for Indian nationalist students. Very soon, he emerged as the leader of a passionate group of revolutionaries based there. In May 1907, Savarkar organized events in London to mark the fiftieth anniversary of the 1857 uprising. He also sent to India a series of fiery pamphlets titled 'Oh Martyrs', which honoured those who had died fighting on the rebel side during the 1857 rebellion. While living in England, Vinayak Savarkar also undertook the task of translating the autobiography of Italian revolutionary Giuseppe Mazzini, titled *Life and Writings of Joseph Mazzini*, from English into Marathi. In addition to translating the text, Savarkar wrote a comprehensive introduction that explained Mazzini's political ideals. He emphasized the need for elevating political engagement to the level of sacred duty and drew a compelling parallel between Mazzini and the revered

Saint Ramdas of Maharashtra, asserting that both figures embodied a shared spiritual and nationalist vision, albeit under different names. Savarkar particularly underscored Mazzini's role in inspiring the youth to fight for national liberation. Once the translation was complete, he sent the manuscript to India for publication. Upon its release, the Marathi edition was met with overwhelming enthusiasm, with all copies of the first edition selling out rapidly. During his stay, Savarkar completed a work in Marathi titled *The Indian War of Independence, 1857* offering his perspective on the 1857 revolt, which he refused to label as a mutiny. As soon as the book reached India and its publication came to the notice of the British authorities, it was immediately banned by the government.

Vinayak Savarkar's involvement with revolutionary activities went beyond just speeches and writings. In 1908, when his cook, Chaturbhuj, was returning to India from London, Savarkar instructed him to conceal a parcel in his trunk. This parcel contained 20 Browning pistols and some 200 quantities of cartridges, meant to be delivered in Bombay for use in revolutionary activities. Originally, these pistols were intended for Ganesh Savarkar in Nasik, who was aware of their impending arrival through Chaturbhuj. However, before they could reach him, Ganesh Savarkar got arrested. As a result, an alternate arrangement was made. Upon arrival in Bombay, the pistols were collected by Gopal Krishna Patankar. Although Ganesh Savarkar had clearly instructed that the pistols should not be sent to Nasik, this order was ignored. Patankar later handed over five pistols and some cartridges to K.G. Karve, one of the conspirators in Mr Jackson's assassination, without any payment.

As discussed in the trial of Anant Laxman Kanhere, Karve through G.V. Vaidya passed one of these pistols to Anant, which was ultimately used in the assassination of Mr Jackson, District Collector of Nasik.

THE TRIAL

In the High Court of Judicature at Bombay
Judgment of Special Tribunal
Special Tribunal Case No. 2, 3 and 4 of 1910

During the investigation into the assassination of Mr Jackson, several individuals were arrested. Statements made by the detainees led the authorities to suspect a widespread and organized conspiracy. As inquiries deepened, more people were taken into custody. While some were released, over fifty were presented before the Magistrate for further examination. Among them, seven including Anant Laxman Kanhere were tried and convicted of the murder of Mr Jackson in a separate case that had already concluded. Of the remaining individuals, 35 were formally committed to stand trial for a larger conspiracy case.

Subsequently, Vinayak Damodar Savarkar was extradited from England, brought before a Magistrate, and committed to face trial as well. All the accused were jointly charged with planning and preparing for an armed rebellion under Section 121 of the IPC. They were also accused of conspiring to overthrow the British government using violence or the threat of violence, under Section 121A of the Indian Penal Code. All the accused were represented by legal counsel, except Savarkar, who chose not to engage a lawyer to defend himself.

The prosecution submitted several pieces of evidence before the court to support its case. These included inflammatory speeches allegedly delivered by Vinayak and his younger brother, Narayan Savarkar, as well as by Mahadev Bhat. Additionally, the prosecution presented a photograph featuring several members of the Mitra Mela, many of whom were among the accused grouped around Vinayak Savarkar. In the photograph, multiple portraits of Shivaji, a board displaying the slogan 'Vande Mataram', and a book titled after Mazzini were clearly visible. These items were presented to corroborate witness testimonies about the objectives and methods of the association. To establish the charge of political conspiracy under Section 121A of the Indian Penal Code, the prosecution relied on various forms of evidence like testimonies from approvers, proof of inflammatory and seditious speeches delivered by the accused, the printing and circulation of revolutionary literature, confessional statements made by the accused, etc.

In response, the defence argued that a conspiracy under Section 121A required a shared understanding or joint objective among all accused individuals. However, in this case, many of the accused had no acquaintance with one another. The defence contended that if they were unaware of each other's existence, they could not have participated in a coordinated conspiracy. According to their argument, the evidence merely suggested the existence of several small and disconnected groups, each possibly working with revolutionary aims but without any unified plan. Therefore, they claimed, the prosecution had failed to prove a single, collective conspiracy involving all the accused.

Findings of the Court

A total of 69 hearings were conducted during the course of the trial. In delivering its verdict on 23 December 1910, three judges (Chief Justice Basil Scott, Justice Chandavarkar and Justice Heaton) of the Special Court rejected the defence's argument that a conspiracy required every accused individual to have made a direct agreement with all others involved. The court clarified that, under the law, it was sufficient for a person to be part of a broader group that planned the crime, even if they did not personally communicate with the individual who executed it.

The court further emphasized that a formal organization among conspirators was not essential. What mattered was the existence of a shared objective and the willingness of individuals to support one another in achieving it. This conclusion was reinforced by the conduct of the accused when, for example, Ganesh Savarkar was arrested, and documents and explosive materials were quickly destroyed or hidden in Nasik by individuals from another group who did not even know him personally. The court finally concluded that the actions of the accused in the present case fell clearly within the scope of Section 121A of the Indian Penal Code, which dealt with criminal conspiracy to wage war against the King.

Finding of the Court vis-à-vis V.D. Savarkar

In the opinion of the Special Court, undoubtedly Vinayak Damodar Savarkar was the central figure or the most significant accused in the entire trial. Accordingly, while examining Savarkar's case separately, the court made specific mention of a letter allegedly written by him on the occasion of the 50th anniversary of the Indian Mutiny, commemorated in London. The court interpreted this letter as a forceful declaration of war towards the British government. Notably, three lines from this letter were explicitly cited in the judgment as illustrative of Savarkar's revolutionary intent:

> The war began on the 10th of May 1857 is not over on the 10th of May 1908, nor shall it ever cease till a 10th of May to come sees the destiny accomplished.

Out of the 35 individuals committed to stand trial under Sections 121 and 121A of the Indian Penal Code, the court ultimately convicted 27, issuing sentences based on their respective roles in the conspiracy. From the outset, it was clear that the British colonial administration viewed Vinayak Damodar Savarkar as its primary adversary and the British court, seemingly aligning with this perception, imposed upon him the harshest sentence among all the accused. Savarkar was found guilty of abetting the waging of war against the King-Emperor through the dissemination of seditious literature, through distribution of arms and by circulating detailed instructions on the manufacture of explosives. Accordingly, the court convicted him under Section 121 of the IPC for abetment of war against the sovereign. In addition, he was also found guilty under Section 121A for conspiring, along with others, to overawe the Government of India by use of criminal force. Here is the list of all the accused who were committed to trial before the Special Court, along with the sentences imposed on them following the conclusion of the trial:

Sr. No.	*Accused*	*Status after trial*
1	Vinayak Kashinath Gaidhani	Acquitted and discharged
2	Ramchandra Babaji Kathe	Acquitted and discharged
3	Govind Sadashiv Bapat	Acquitted and discharged
4	Hari Anant Thatte	Acquitted and discharged
5	Shankar Pandurang Mahajan	Acquitted and discharged
6	Mukund Pandurang Moghe	Acquitted and discharged
7	Keshav Ganesh Paranjpe	Acquitted and discharged
8	Trimbak Vinayak Jog	Acquitted and discharged
9	Vinayak Damodar Savarkar	Transportation for life and forfeiture of all his property
10	Keshav Shripat Chandwadkar	Transportation for 15 years
11	Gopal Krishna Patankar	Rigorously imprisoned for 10 years
12	Krishnaji Gopal Khare,	Rigorously imprisoned for 10 years
13	Trimbak Gangadhar Marathe	Rigorously imprisoned for 10 years
14	Vyankatesh Parashram Nagpurkar	Rigorously imprisoned for 7 years
15	Vishnu Mahadev Bhat	Rigorously imprisoned for 5 years
16	Purshottam Laxman Dandekar	Rigorously imprisoned for 5 years

Sr. No.	*Accused*	*Status after trial*
17	Damodar Mahadev Chandratre	Rigorously imprisoned for 5 years
18	Sakharam Dadaji Gorhe	Rigorously imprisoned for 5 years
19	Gopal Govind Dharap	Rigorously imprisoned for 5 years
20	Shridhar Vasudev Shidhaye	Rigorously imprisoned for 4 years
21	Raghunath Vidhyadhar Bhave	Rigorously imprisoned for 4 years
22	Damodar Chintaman Paranjpe	Rigorously imprisoned for 4 years
23	Vaman Kashinath Palande	Rigorously imprisoned for 4 years
24	Vishnu Ganesh Kelkar	Rigorously imprisoned for 3 years
25	Kashinath Daji Tonpe	Rigorously imprisoned for 3 years
26	Parashram Vaman Gokhale	Rigorously imprisoned for 3 years
27	Anant Vishnu Konkar	Rigorously imprisoned for 3 years
28	Vishwas Balwant Dawre	Rigorously imprisoned for 3 years
29	Vinayak Govind Tikhe	Rigorously imprisoned for 2 years

Sr. No.	*Accused*	*Status after trial*
30	Balwant Ramchandra Barve	Rigorously imprisoned for 2 years
31	Sakharam Rangnath Kashikar	Rigorously imprisoned for 2 years
32	Narayan Damodar Savarkar	Rigorously imprisoned for 6 months
33	Vinayak Vasudev Manohar	Rigorously imprisoned for 6 months
34	Gangaram Rupchand	Rigorously imprisoned for 6 months
35	Raghunath Chintaman Ambdekar	Rigorously imprisoned for 6 months

Second Trial of Vinayak Damodar Savarkar

The British government sought to prosecute Vinayak Damodar Savarkar not only on charges of criminal conspiracy but also for abetment of the murder of Mr A.M.T. Jackson, the District Collector of Nasik. According to the prosecution, the pistol used by Anant Laxman Kanhere in the assassination of Mr Jackson on 21 December 1909 had allegedly been supplied by Savarkar from England. Consequently, on 10 September 1910, Savarkar was formally committed for trial before a Special Tribunal comprising judges of the Bombay High Court, to face charges of abetment of murder under Sections 109 and 302 of the Indian Penal Code. The central issue in this trial revolved around the allegation that Savarkar had dispatched the pistols used in the murder, thereby necessitating judicial determination of whether he was guilty of abetment of murder.

In the High Court of Judicature at Bombay
Special Bench Case No. 1 of 1911
Emperor v. Vinayak Damodar Savarkar

According to the prosecution, Ganesh Savarkar was aware that Chaturbhuj was bringing pistols from England. He conveyed this information to his associate, Gopal Krishna Patankar. In accordance with the instructions received, Chaturbhuj delivered the pistols and a letter to Patankar shortly after Ganesh Savarkar's arrest. To avoid detection by the authorities, Patankar decided to transfer a portion of the consignment to K.G. Karve, a close acquaintance with whom he frequently discussed nationalist ideas. Karve initially received five pistols from Patankar—two large and three small, followed later by two more—along with matching ammunition. These weapons, smuggled in by Chaturbhuj, were then transported by Karve to Nasik. Over time, he distributed the pistols among his associates. When his group eventually resolved to assassinate District Magistrate A.M.T. Jackson, incensed by the role he played in committing Ganesh Savarkar to trial, one of the large pistols was handed over to Anant Laxman Kanhere, who had been selected to carry out the murder. On the evening of 21 December 1909, in a crowded theatre in Nasik, Kanhere fatally shot Mr Jackson using that very pistol.

Finding of the Court

In his second trial, Vinayak Savarkar once again chose not to engage legal counsel but addressed the court personally at the end of the proceedings. He denied any association with Anant Laxman Kanhere or members of Karve's group, and argued that when the pistols were allegedly sent from England, his brother Ganesh Savarkar had not yet been charged. Therefore, he claimed, the prosecution's theory that the pistols were sent to avenge Ganesh's prosecution was unfounded. Without that motive, Savarkar argued, Mr Jackson's assassination could not have been the intended outcome, and thus he should not be held liable for abetment. However, the Special Court rejected these arguments in its verdict dated 3 February 1911. It ruled that even if Ganesh's prosecution had not begun at the time, Savarkar's act of sending weapons for use against officials still made him culpable. The court held that responsibility was not negated simply because only one targeted individual was ultimately killed. It found that Savarkar was part of a larger conspiracy to commit violent acts against government officials, and sending the shipment of pistols was a key step in executing that plan. Mr Jackson's murder was seen as a direct result of this conspiracy. Furthermore, the court rejected the claim that Savarkar couldn't be held responsible because he did not personally know the assassins. Citing Explanation 5 of Section 108 of the Indian Penal Code, it stated that direct communication between the abettor and the perpetrator was not necessary; involvement in a conspiracy that led to the crime was sufficient for criminal liability. Significantly, the life sentence awarded in this trial was ordered to begin only after the completion of the earlier sentence, not concurrently. Thus, with two consecutive life sentences, the British effectively condemned Savarkar to fifty years of imprisonment in the Andamans.

Aftermath

Though Savarkar remains a debated figure in Indian history, his contribution to the country's freedom struggle is undeniably significant. His sacrifices and determination, despite immense personal hardship, inspired countless others to join the fight for independence. The judgment in Savarkar's first trial was notably lengthy, offering a comprehensive account of his involvement in India's freedom movement from his early school days to his activities in London. In many respects, it serves as a significant historical document that reflects Savarkar's unwavering patriotic fervour. In 1921, Savarkar was transferred from the Andaman Islands to the Indian mainland and was held in Ratnagiri Jail until 1924. Upon his release that year, his movements remained restricted, as he was confined to Ratnagiri District. While in prison, he authored his renowned book, *Hindutva: Who Is a Hindu?* After his release from prison, Savarkar also assumed leadership of the Hindu Mahasabha, an organization advocating the cause of Hindus.

EIGHT

TRIAL OF BASANT BISWAS (DELHI-LAHORE CONSPIRACY CASE)

When Lord Hardinge, Governor-General of India (1910–16), arrived at Delhi Railway Station on 23 December 1912, he was received by the ruling princes of India and other high-ranking British officials. In 1912, preparations were in full swing for shifting the capital from Calcutta to Delhi. British officials felt comparatively relaxed in Delhi as Calcutta (existing capital) was the epicentre of all revolutionaries' activities and hence Delhi was less hostile for them. After deboarding from the train, Lord Hardinge and his wife mounted two different elephants. Governor-General and Lady Hardinge sat on a silver howdah and their grand procession started moving from the railway station to the main market of Chandni Chowk. It was a perfect morning and the procession of elephants made a most striking picture of oriental colour and splendour.[61]

Somehow, Lord Hardinge had a premonition that something bad was going to happen and he shared this feeling with his wife. But his wife thought it was his dislike for crowded ceremonial functions which was making him uncomfortable.

[61]Lord Hardinge, *My Indian Years, 1910–1916*, John Murray, London.

As the procession moved further into the walled city, an explosion took place. The Governor-General's elephant stopped and his helmet fell down from his head. It took him a few seconds to realize that there had been a bomb attack. He glanced towards his wife, who was on another elephant, to check whether she was ok or not. While Lady Hardinge was ok, the Governor-General had been badly injured in the bomb attack. His servant who was sitting just behind him and who was holding the state umbrella had died instantly and his body got entangled in the ropes of the howdah. The Governor-General fainted after a few minutes because of the loss of blood and regained his senses only after receiving first aid. The sound of the explosion had been so loud that it was heard from six miles away.

Rash Bihari Bose and Basant Kumar Biswas were the two revolutionaries behind this bomb attack on the Governor-General. Their objective was to assassinate Lord Hardinge in order to send a clear message to the British that their rule in India was nearing its end. Although they failed in their attempt as Lord Hardinge survived in the bomb attack, they managed to escape from the scene by taking advantage of the large crowd. Interestingly, Rash Bihari Bose, who planned this attack, was at that time a government servant, working as a clerk at the Forest Research Institute (FRI) in Dehradun.

Basant Kumar Biswas, an expert bomb-maker, played a key role in the operation. He had been mentored by Rash Bihari Bose and brought from Bengal to Dehradun under his guidance. Rash Bihari Bose was an exceptionally shrewd revolutionary. Despite being a government employee, he was able to organize underground revolutionary activities without ever falling under the suspicion of the CID or police authorities.

Just a few days after the bombing, he even organized a public meeting in Dehradun to condemn the attack. When Lord Hardinge later visited Dehradun, Rash Bihari Bose led a group of British loyalists and publicly pledged his allegiance to the British government. Governor-General Lord Hardinge, in his memoir *My Indian Years*, recalls his meeting with Rash Bihari Bose in the following words:

> Two incidents of interest occurred on the journey, one of them being apparent only some months later. The first was that a wild elephant stood on the railway track and for sometime refused to move, threatening to attack the engine. The second was that when driving in a car from the station to my bungalow, I passed an Indian standing in front of the gate of his house with several others, all of whom were very demonstrative in their salaams. On my inquiring who these people might be I was told that the principal Indian there had presided two days before at a public meeting at Dehradun and had proposed and carried a vote of condolence with me on account of the attack on my life. It was proved later that it was this identical Indian who threw the bomb at me.

When Har Dayal, a renowned Indian revolutionary and freedom fighter, left for America, revolutionary work in North India was taken up by Amir Chand, a respected teacher at the Cambridge Mission School in Delhi, and Rash Bihari Bose. These two soon emerged as key figures in India's revolutionary movement, which included several Bengalis among its active participants. The revolutionaries primarily sourced their funds and explosives from Bengal. At that time, it was extremely rare and dangerous for a government servant to be involved in revolutionary activities. Such involvement could result not only in the loss of job but also in the ultimate penalty which was death by execution.

Despite the risks, Rash Bihari Bose not only continued his covert work but also built a committed team of revolutionaries who were ready to sacrifice everything for their country. This team led by Rash Bihari Bose was primarily divided into two groups: the Lahore group and the Delhi group. The Lahore group comprised Dina Nath, Balmokand and Bal Raj, while the Delhi group included Amir Chand, Hanumant Sahai and Abad Bihari. Abad Bihari acted as the link between the two groups.

In a meeting held at Lahore in October 1912, this team of revolutionaries under the leadership of Rash Bihari Bose decided to publish an anonymous leaflet titled 'Liberty', with the aim of inciting public discontent against the British government. Rash Bihari entrusted the task of writing the leaflet to Abad Bihari, who, like a loyal and obedient soldier, not only wrote it but also ensured its publication in Kapurthala. Subsequently, thousands of 'Liberty' leaflets were widely distributed across northern India. This leaflet called for revolution and demanded complete independence from British rule. Below are the key excerpts from this historic document:

> Revolution has never been the work of men. It is always God's own will worked through instruments. Those who are commissioned to bring about mighty changes were full of the force of Zeitgeist. Spirit enters into them. God Himself worked through Khudi Ram Bose, Prafulla Chaki, Kanai Lal Dutt, Madan Lal Dhingra and others. The thrower of bomb on the representative of the

> tyrannical Government at Delhi was none else but the spirit of the Dispenser of all things Himself [...] The debt we owe to the noble spirits of the martyrs will be paid only when young men of India will begin to come forward in numbers, each to prove a worthy successor of these departed sons [...]
>
> A grim Revolution is the greatest need of the times. Rise, brothers, in spirit. Individual incidents like the one at Delhi may strike terrors into the hearts of the tyrants but they cannot bring you the desired goal. They are helpful to a very great extent; but let us not forget the end and should lose no time for the real work. Let us be up and doing for the great work of Revolution, our cherished ideal.

In furtherance of their revolutionary activities after the bomb attack on Governor-General, Rash Bihari Bose and his team decided to assassinate Mr Gordon, former sub-divisional officer of Sylhet, under whose order the police raid on the ashram of Swami Dayananda was conducted. Mr Gordon was expected to be at a bar in Lawrence Gardens, Lahore, on 17 May 1913. Basant Kumar Biswas was assigned the task of throwing a bomb at the location.

However, at the last moment, he lost his nerve and instead of placing the bomb in Lawrence Gardens, he threw it onto the road. Tragically, an Indian orderly named Ram Padarath, riding his bicycle in the dark, accidentally ran over the bomb and was killed. A few days later, during the CID investigation into the Lawrence Gardens bombing, authorities discovered a link between the Lahore bombing and the earlier Delhi bombing. As the investigation progressed, the entire conspiracy was unravelled by the CID. An FIR was filed against

Rash Bihari Bose, Lala Hanumant Sahai, Bhai Balmokand, Amir Chand, Awadh Bihari, Basant Kumar Biswas, etc. The case came to be known as the Delhi-Lahore Conspiracy Case.

THE TRIAL

The Crown v. Basant Kumar Biswas & Ors.

Trial No. 6 of 1914

Judge: Mr M. Harrison, Additional Session Judge, Delhi

Although the CID did not find any concrete evidence in connection with the Delhi bombing, certain clues emerged from the Lahore bomb incident. As a result, a conspiracy case was instituted in 1914 against eleven individuals. The evidence against the accused in the Delhi bomb case were entirely circumstantial and centred around the fact that Basant Kumar Biswas had left Lahore just a few days before the bombing under suspicious circumstances and Abad Bihari was also absent from Lahore at that time.

Unfortunately, one of the revolutionaries, Dina Nath (PW3), turned approver. Based on the information he provided, the Delhi-Lahore Conspiracy Trial commenced on 21 May 1914 and continued until 1 September 1914. In his court testimony, Dina Nath claimed that he had had a conversation with Abad Bihari, during which Abad Bihari had confessed to knowing the details of how the bomb was thrown on Lord Hardinge in Delhi. All the accused were charged under Sections 302 and 120B of the Indian Penal Code for conspiracy to commit murder in both the Delhi and Lahore incidents. Additionally, they were charged under Sections 4, 5 and 6 of the Explosive Substances Act. The prosecution relied on the testimony of 203 witnesses and submitted 252 bundles of exhibits. The first act of the conspiracy was said to be the bombing on the Governor-General of India in Delhi on 23 December 1912.

On 5 October 1914, the trial court delivered its verdict and sentenced Amir Chand, Abad Bihari and Balmokand to death. The trial court dealt with the case of each accused separately in its order. While awarding punishment, a distinction was drawn between those who actually handled bombs and those who did not, or who were not shown to have done so. The first class included Basant Kumar Biswas, Abad Bihari, Amir Chand and Balmokand while the latter, Bal Raj and Hanumant Sahai. Below is the court's summary of the role played by each accused and the corresponding sentence awarded to them.

(i) **Basant Kumar Biswas:** Basant Kumar Biswas had handled bombs on more than one occasion. Although the court acknowledged that he was indeed the one who had planted the bomb that caused the death of Ram Padarath (orderly) and was intended to inflict further casualties, it was inclined to treat him with leniency. The court noted that Basant was only 23 years old and was less developed both mentally and physically than what was typically expected at that age. The court further observed that Basant came from a very humble background and had served as a domestic help to the dominant revolutionary leader Rash Bihari Bose. Socially and educationally, he was not on par with his fellow conspirators. It was also noted that Basant was never admitted into the core leadership or inner circle of the revolutionary committee. While he clearly understood the nature of his actions, the court believed he merited more compassion than those who trained, guided and exploited him. Therefore, despite being directly responsible for the murder of Ram Padarath, the court sentenced him to transportation for life under Section 302 read with Section 120B of the Indian Penal Code.

(ii) **Abad Bihari:** Abad Bihari was only 25 years old but was a highly educated and intelligent man, as observed by the court. From the very beginning, he was an active member of the committee, involved in planning and consulted on every matter. Although he did not personally place the bomb in Lahore, he chose to entrust this dangerous task to Basant Kumar Biswas. He also organized the leaflet campaign, which was intended to incite acts of violence and crime. Notably, he was found in possession of the Poison Manual. The court awarded him the maximum punishment prescribed by law. Under Section 302 read with Section 120B of the Indian Penal Code, he was sentenced to death.

(iii) **Amir Chand:** Amir Chand was a 40-year-old man and a respected figure in Delhi's educational circles. He was frequently consulted by his fellow revolutionaries and was known for using his remarkable talents and influence over the youth to inspire them to join revolution. He allegedly authored an article advocating the wholesale massacre of Europeans. Furthermore, he allowed his house in Delhi to be used as a central meeting place for revolutionaries. A portion of a bomb was later discovered there by the police. He was found guilty under Sections 302 and 120B of the Indian Penal Code and was sentenced to death by the court.

(iv) **Balmokand:** Balmokand was a founding member of the

committee led by Rash Bihari Bose which was responsible for making all major decisions, including those related to the Lahore bombing. He was in possession of all the bombs brought from Bengal by Basant Kumar, and whenever he was in Lahore, he actively participated in the committee's operations. His correspondence clearly demonstrated that he was fully aware of his actions. The court found him guilty under Sections 302 and 120B of the Indian Penal Code and sentenced him to death.

(v) **Balraj:** Balraj, unlike his friend, was not shown to have ever actually handled a bomb. However, he was equally guilty as his friend Balmokand, being an active member of the conspiracy. The court drew a distinction in terms of punishment in Balraj's case. It observed that although Balraj was undoubtedly a full member from the beginning and a part of the managing committee, justice would be served by sentencing him to transportation for life. Accordingly, the court found Balraj guilty under Sections 302 and 120B of the Indian Penal Code and passed this sentence.

(vi) **Hanumant Sahai:** Hanumant Sahai was also an active member of the group, but the prosecution failed to establish that he played any prominent role in executing the actual act of violence. This became a significant factor that the court considered while determining his sentence. He was found guilty under Sections 302 and 120B of the Indian Penal Code for being part of the conspiracy and was sentenced to transportation for life.

(vii) **Dina Nath:** Dina Nath was an active member of the group, but after being arrested by the police, he succumbed to pressure and turned government approver. He revealed all information related to the revolutionaries. In return for turning approver, the court granted him a pardon and formally discharged him from the case.

Sr. No.	*Accused*	*Punishment*
1	Rash Bihari Bose	Absconded
2	Dina Nath	Pardon as he became approver
3	Amir Chand	Death sentence
4	Abad Bihari	Death sentence
5	Basant Kumar Biswas	Transported for life but on appeal by the government he was hanged
6	Balmokand	Death sentence
7	Balraj	Transported for life
8	Hanumant Sahai	Transported for life

Aftermath

Due to his young age, Basant Kumar Biswas was initially sentenced to life imprisonment. However, following an appeal filed by the British government, Lahore High Court awarded him the death penalty. He was hanged on 11 May 1915. After some time, Rash Bihari Bose managed to escape to Japan, where he lived in exile until his death. Even in exile, he continued to work tirelessly for the cause of India's independence. Upon reaching Japan, he immediately began the second phase of his revolutionary activities. This phase eventually culminated in the formation of the Indian Independence League and the Azad Hind Fauj (Indian National Army), which was later led by Subhas Chandra Bose.

While writing about the Delhi Conspiracy Case, Michael O'Dwyer, in his book *India as I Knew it*,[62] states:

> Among the key figures in the broader movement were the notorious Har Dayal, a Punjabi who later advanced the cause in America, and an equally dangerous conspirator, Rash Bihari Bose, a Bengali who served as the head clerk in a government office in Dehradun. These individuals drew several others into the conspiracy primarily students, but also some men of status and mature age.

The Lahore-Delhi Conspiracy Case holds considerable significance, as it served as a catalyst for the British administration to bring about substantial changes in the Indian Penal Code (IPC) and the CrPC. Prior to 1913, criminal conspiracy was punishable only if it resulted in the commission of an illegal act. However, in the aftermath of the Delhi-Lahore Conspiracy Case, the British colonial government recognized the need to criminalize even the mere agreement to commit an illegal act, regardless of whether the act was ultimately carried out or not. Accordingly, the Criminal Law Amendment Act of 1913 introduced Sections 120A and 120B into the IPC, thereby making criminal conspiracy a separate and punishable offence, in certain cases even without any overt act being committed. While Section 120A defines the offence of criminal conspiracy, Section 120B lays down the punishment for such an offence.

---

[62] *India as I Knew It* is a memoir by Sir Michael O'Dwyer, an Indian Civil Service officer who served as the Lieutenant Governor of Punjab from 1913 to 1919 during British rule in India.

NINE

TRIAL OF SACHINDRA NATH SANYAL (THE BANARAS CONSPIRACY CASE)

A national flag having four colours (representing the four different religions of India) was designed, uniform shorts were made for the mutineers, a list of vehicles was prepared to transport people, and rations for several people were arranged in advance. Sachindra Nath Sanyal, Rash Bihari Bose and their fellow revolutionaries were meticulously planning for the uprising against the British government scheduled on 21 February 1915. According to their plan, Indian soldiers from different cantonments across North India would launch a surprise attack on the British troops stationed in those cantonments. British soldiers who would surrender would be taken as prisoners.

The attack was to begin at night and electricity would be cut off. The treasury would be seized and jails would be broken into to free prisoners, and the city's administration would be taken over by the revolutionaries. Though Sachindra Nath Sanyal and Rash Bihari Bose were fully aware of the enormity of the challenge, they believed that if their strategy was executed effectively and they received support from foreign nations hostile to the British, achieving India's independence though difficult would not be impossible.[63] While Rash Bihari Bose took charge of the preparations in Lahore, Sachindra Nath Sanyal oversaw the Indian soldiers stationed at the cantonment in Kashi. However, the British government had managed to place a mole named Kripal Singh among the revolutionaries, who passed all the information about the planned uprising to the police. When the revolutionaries in Lahore learned that their plan had been compromised, they brought the date of the uprising forward. With Rash Bihari Bose's consent, the attack was rescheduled to take place on 19 February instead of 21 February 1915. However, the police were already alerted and, prior to 19 February, approximately 200 revolutionaries were arrested across North India, thwarting the planned uprising. Many arrests occurred in Banaras, where a special court was established under the Defence of India Act, 1915, to try these accused. This judicial proceeding came to be known as the Banaras Conspiracy Case.

We have already discussed Rash Bihari Bose in chapter eight of this book. This chapter, however, focuses on the Banaras Conspiracy Case, in which Sachindra Nath Sanyal was the principal accused. Sachindra Nath Sanyal was a prominent Indian revolutionary and founder of the HRA, which was later renamed Hindustan Socialist Republican Association (HSRA) by Bhagat Singh in 1928. He played a crucial role in organizing armed resistance against British colonial rule and served as a mentor to several young revolutionaries, including Chandrashekhar Azad, Jatindra Nath Das and Bhagat Singh. Sachindra Nath Sanyal and his family used to reside in Banaras.

---

[63]Sanyal, Sachindra Nath, *Bandi Jeevan: A Life in Chains*, translated by Sanjeev Sanyal, Rupa Publications, New Delhi, 2023.

Originally from Bengal, Sanyal studied at Bengali Tola Inter College in Varanasi. Along with his schoolmates, he founded a club in Banaras, initially named Anushilan Samiti, inspired by the revolutionary organization of the same name in Bengal.

However, recognizing the legal risks associated with that name, the group soon renamed itself Young Men's Association. The Association claimed to promote the moral, intellectual and physical development of its members. According to Bibhuti, a former revolutionary and friend of Sanyal, who later turned into a government approver in the Banaras Conspiracy Case, the Association had an inner circle whose members were fully aware of its true objectives. Revolutionary ideology was secretly imparted during so-called 'moral classes', in which texts like the Bhagavad Gita were interpreted in a way that justified acts of political assassination. During the annual Kali Puja, the group would perform a ritual involving the sacrifice of a white pumpkin—a gesture that, although traditionally innocuous, was symbolically used to represent the sacrifice of the white race, while special prayers were offered for its expulsion from India.

Before the establishment of the Anushilan Samiti in Banaras, the city had already been visited by several revolutionaries from Bengal who left a deep impression on the local youth. Evidently Sachindra Nath Sanyal and his associates, mainly Bengalis, were profoundly influenced by these earlier revolutionary figures. Sachindra Nath Sanyal was a close associate of Rash Bihari Bose and holds the rare distinction of being the first revolutionary to be deported twice to Kala Pani to serve life imprisonment. His first deportation followed his conviction in the Banaras Conspiracy Case. However, after the end of World War I, he was released under a general amnesty programme.

THE TRIAL

Special Tribunal Constituted under Defence of India Act, 1915
Date of Judgment: 14 February 1916

Judges: S.R. Daniels, B.J. Dalal and Sitla Prasad Bajpai

Counsel for the accused: B.C. Chatterjee

The Banaras Conspiracy Case was a major criminal trial during British rule in India, held in the early 20th century. It formed part of the colonial government's efforts to suppress the growing wave of revolutionary nationalism. The case revolved around events that took place around 1915, during World War I, a time when the British were particularly anxious about internal uprisings. This case was closely linked to the Ghadar Movement.[64]

Inspired by the Ghadar Movement, many revolutionaries returned to India from the US and other Western countries, hoping to spark mutinies within the Indian Army, especially in Punjab and Uttar Pradesh. The British authorities treated the case as one of the most serious instances of sedition, placing it alongside landmark trials like the Alipore Bomb Case and the Lahore Conspiracy Case in terms of its significance and impact. The Banaras Conspiracy Case was initiated against 15 accused. Out of the 24 individuals against whom prosecution was sanctioned, 15 were presented before the court, while the remaining nine, including Rash Bihari Bose, were declared absconders. They were later brought before a Special Tribunal

[64]A revolutionary effort led by Indian expatriates mostly based in North America who aimed to trigger an armed revolt against British rule.

comprising three judges, constituted under the Defence of India Act.

The charges framed against Sachindra Nath Sanyal, his brother Jatinder Nath Sanyal and thirteen others included serious offences under various sections (Sections 121, 121A, 122 and 131) of the Indian Penal Code, primarily for waging war against the King-Emperor, sedition, and conspiracy to overthrow the British government. During police raids, explosives, arms and seditious publications were reportedly recovered from the accused. The prosecution's case relied heavily on the statements of the approvers and on documents purportedly linking the accused to foreign agents and revolutionary activities. In contrast to the earlier conspiracy cases at Delhi and Lahore, the evidence in this case did not point to any actual acts of violence such as murders, robberies or bombings. The activities attributed to the Banaras faction of the conspiracy were limited to:

(i) Circulating seditious literature;
(ii) Attempting to instigate the Indian troops to rebel; and
(iii) Functioning as a supply centre for bombs and ammunition being sent from Bengal and other regions to revolutionary groups in Meerut, Delhi and Punjab.

Facts of the Case

In the autumn of 1913, Sachindra Nath Sanyal and his associates began circulating seditious pamphlets among school and college students in Banaras. Some of these were also distributed by post. They frequently visited nearby villages, delivering speeches aimed at inciting disaffection against British rule and awakening the political consciousness of the rural population. Around this time, following the Delhi-Lahore

Conspiracy Case, the British government had announced a reward of ₹10,000 for the arrest of the elusive Rash Bihari Bose, whose photograph was widely circulated. Despite these efforts, Rash Bihari remained untraceable.

In early 1914, Rash Bihari Bose secretly arrived in Banaras and remained there for much of the year, successfully evading detection by the police and intelligence services. During his stay, he assumed leadership of the revolutionary movement in the city. Under his command, Sanyal and his fellow revolutionaries set their sights on overthrowing British rule through armed insurrection. The literature they distributed, such as the 'Swadhin Bharat' and 'Liberty' leaflets, was openly revolutionary and explicitly called for rebellion and political assassinations. Between 1914 and 1915, Sachindra Nath Sanyal made several visits to the cantonment of the 7th Rajputana regiment in Banaras. Working in coordination with Lahore-based revolutionaries like Pingley and Sucha Singh, as well as with Bibhuti, who would later turn approver, he attempted on multiple occasions to sway the loyalty of Indian soldiers stationed at Banaras and to incite them to revolt on a predetermined date. Sachindra Nath Sanyal and his associates frequently visited Rash Bihari Bose at his residence in Banaras, where he regularly demonstrated how bombs and revolvers were to be handled and used.

On the night of 18 November 1914, during one such session, an accidental explosion occurred while Rash Bihari was handling explosives, which injured both him and Sanyal. In the aftermath, Bose promptly shifted his residence to another location in the city. When questioned by neighbours about the blast, they were misleadingly told that a soda water bottle had burst. Following Rash Bihari's instructions,

Sachindra Nath Sanyal and Vishnu Ganesh Pingley travelled to Punjab, where they established contact with several Ghadar Party revolutionaries. Soon after, Rash Bihari Bose declared that a widespread armed uprising was imminent and urged his followers to be prepared to sacrifice their lives for the nation. Explosives and firearms were brought in from Bengal to support the plan. Revolutionaries like Bibhuti and Priya Nath were tasked with visiting different military cantonments to incite soldiers to revolt on a pre-decided date.

Acting under the leadership of Rash Bihari Bose, a plan was drawn up to launch a coordinated uprising on 21 February 1915 across several key military cantonments in northern India. While Rash Bihari took charge of operations in Lahore, Sachindra Nath Sanyal was assigned responsibility for Banaras, where he anticipated support from the 7th Rajputana regiment. However, the revolutionary network in Lahore soon discovered that their plans had been compromised, which prompted them to bring forward the date of the revolt to 19 February 1915. Several soldiers stationed at cantonments across Punjab and Delhi had agreed to participate in the uprising. Unfortunately, a police informant named Kirpal Singh betrayed the plot, leading to widespread arrests in Punjab, Delhi and other regions before the date fixed for the revolt.

Unaware of the revised date, the revolutionaries in Banaras, led by Sachindra Nath Sanyal, assembled on the parade ground of the local cantonment on the evening of 21 February, awaiting a revolt that never came. When nothing happened on the fixed date, Sachindra Nath Sanyal went to Kashi railway station to find our whether trains and telegraph were working or if there had been any disruptions. To Sachindra Nath, disruption in the railway and telegraph network signified that something was afoot. But to their surprise everything was working fine. Sanyal bought a newspaper from the platform and saw that arrests had begun in Lahore. He realized that things had not gone according to plan and he made the decision to leave the city immediately.

By that time, the conspiracy had already been uncovered in Lahore, and numerous revolutionaries were arrested. Rash Bihari Bose and Vishnu Ganesh Pingley briefly returned to Banaras before Pingley proceeded to Meerut with a supply of bombs. He was arrested there on 23 March and was later sentenced to death. Following the collapse of the planned armed uprising, India was no longer a safe haven for Rash Bihari Bose. He decided to flee the country, but not before holding a final meeting in Calcutta with a few of his close disciples from Banaras.

In his absence, the revolutionary movement was to continue under the leadership of Sachindra Nath Sanyal and Nagendra Nath Datta, also known as Girija Babu, a seasoned revolutionary from eastern Bengal and a former member of the Dacca Anushilan Samiti.

Arrest of Sachindra Nath Sanyal

Subsequent to Rash Bihari's departure to Japan, Sachindra Nath Sanyal was arrested on 26 June 1915 and brought to trial before a special tribunal in Banaras. Sanyal was apprehended by one police officer named Scott O'Connor while he and Bibhuti were in the process of preparing seditious pamphlets for postal distribution. During the investigation into the Banaras Conspiracy Case, several of the accused turned approvers. The prosecution's case largely rested on the testimonies of three key approvers: Bibhuti, Mani Lal and Babu Ram. Among them, the statements provided by Bibhuti and Mani Lal formed the cornerstone of the prosecution's case.

Conviction

One of the most significant pieces of evidence presented during the trial was a copy of *Life of Mazzini* (Exhibit 62), which bore Sachindra Nath Sanyal's name on the title page. This document offered valuable insight into the methods and ideology of Sanyal and his associates. After extensive arguments, the tribunal convicted eleven individuals, sentencing them to long prison terms. Sachindra Nath Sanyal was sentenced to transportation for life in Andaman. The evidence brought before the court substantiated the charges related to attempts to incite disloyalty among troops, the dissemination of seditious literature, and the various conspiratorial activities narrated during the proceedings.

The special tribunal constituted to adjudicate the Banaras Conspiracy Case devoted particular attention to the role of Sachindra Nath Sanyal, whom it described as by far the most dangerous among the accused. He was seen as Rash Bihari Bose's trusted lieutenant in Banaras, and his revolutionary activities were considered broader in scope and more subversive in nature than those of the other co-accused. Sanyal had operated across multiple cities, including Calcutta, Lahore and Amritsar, reflecting the extent of his involvement in the conspiracy. The tribunal found him guilty under Section 121A of the Indian Penal Code for conspiring to wage war against the King and to overthrow British sovereignty in India, and under Section 131, for attempting to incite defection among the soldiers of the 7th Rajputana regiment stationed in the Banaras cantonment. For both offences, he was sentenced to transportation for life, with the sentences to run concurrently.

In addition, he was convicted under Section 122 of the IPC for collection of arms and ammunition with the intent of waging war against the Crown. For this charge too, he was sentenced to transportation for life, which was also supposed to run concurrently with the other sentences. As required under Section 122, the tribunal also ordered the forfeiture of all his property to the government. Following is the list of all 15 accused in the Banaras Conspiracy Case along with the sentences awarded to each of them:

Sr. No.	*Name of Accused*	*Section*	*Punishment*
1	Annada	121A	Rigorous imprisonment for three years
2	Bankim Chandra Mitra	121A	Rigorous imprisonment for three years
3	Damodar Sarup	121A, 122& 511	Rigorous imprisonment for seven years
4	Dharam Singh		Acquitted
5	Jadunath Singh		Acquitted
6	Ganeshi Lal	121A	Rigorous imprisonment for seven years
7	Jitendra Nath Sanyal	121A	Rigorous imprisonment for two years
8	Kalipado Mukherjee	121A	Rigorous imprisonment for three years
9	Nalini Mohan Mukherjee	121A & 131	Rigorous imprisonment for five years
10	Lakshmi Narain	121A	Rigorous imprisonment for five years

Sr. No.	*Name of Accused*	*Section*	*Punishment*
11	Partab Singh	121A	Rigorous imprisonment for five years
12	Rabindra Nath Sanyal		Acquitted
13	Sachindra Nath Sanyal	121A& 131, 122	Transportation for life and forfeiture of property
14	Surendra Nath Mukherjee		Acquitted
15	Girja Babu	121A	Rigorous imprisonment for five years and Rs 500 fine

Aftermath

As a result of the government's confiscation of their property in Banaras, Sachindra Nath Sanyal's family was compelled to leave the city, and they subsequently relocated to Gorakhpur.

The Banaras Conspiracy Case was among several significant trials around the time of World War I that reflected the British government's growing anxiety over coordinated revolutionary activities. Although the immediate goal of the Ghadar Movement to launch a nationwide armed uprising was not realized, the case served as a reminder of the increase in revolutionary activities in the country and the extreme measures Indian nationalists were prepared to adopt in pursuit of independence. The crackdown that followed dealt a serious blow to the revolutionary networks in eastern and northern India, especially in Bengal and the United Provinces.

Sachindra Nath Sanyal was sent to Kala Pani on 18 August

1916 after his brief stay in a Banaras jail subsequent to the court's verdict. As he was given life imprisonment, there was no hope of him coming back soon but luck had something else in store for Sanyal. After World War I was over, he and some other political prisoners were released from the jail in February 1920 under an amnesty scheme of the British government. Sachindra Nath Sanyal came back to Varanasi and once again got involved in revolutionary activities.

Meanwhile he also got married and had two sons. During this period, he founded Hindustan Republican Association (HRA) and drafted its manifesto. The manifesto of the HRA has an important place in the history of the Indian revolutionary movement. Later, when Sachindra Nath Sanyal went to jail, Bhagat Singh renamed this group Hindustan Socialist Republican Association and brought under its umbrella many revolutionary associations. He, however, kept the manifesto unchanged. Sachindra Nath Sanyal was arrested for the second time in 1927 in connection with the Kakori Conspiracy Case[65] and was sentenced to transportation for life. He remained in Cellular Jail until he was released after 10 years in 1937.

When World War II started, Sanyal secretly worked with Japan in order to assist in India's efforts to achieve freedom, and he even guided Subhas Chandra Bose in this regard. But when the British got to know about his plan, he was again arrested and sent to jail where he contracted tuberculosis. He spent his final months in Gorakhpur Jail and died on 6 February 1942 in Gorakhpur. Sachindra Nath Sanyal was the only revolutionary who was involved in almost every phase of India's revolutionary struggle. He was part of the Anushilan

[65]Details of Kakori Conspiracy case are given in *Chapter Six* of this book.

Samiti phase, the Ghadarite and HRA phases, and eventually in the revival during World War II.[66] Sanyal, through the HRA manifesto, was among the first to clearly articulate that post-independence India would be a democratic republic based on universal franchise, at a time when the Indian National Congress was still demanding limited freedom under dominion status.

[66]Sanyal, Sachindra Nath, *Bandi Jeevan*, Atmaram and Sons, Lucknow.

TEN

TRIAL OF MADAN LAL DHINGRA

Lieutenant Colonel Sir William Curzon Wyllie, who once served as the Aide-de-Camp (A.D.C.) to Lord George Hamilton, the Secretary of State for India,[67] had previously held several significant positions in British India. He began his career in the Indian Army and later transferred to the Political Department of the Government of India. Among his prominent appointments were his roles as Military Secretary to the Governor of the Madras Presidency and as the British Resident in Nepal.

During his tenure in India, Curzon Wyllie came into contact with several influential individuals, among them Dr Sahib Dhingra, a respected retired civil surgeon from Punjab. Dr Dhingra had five sons and one of them was Madan Lal Dhingra. Born on 8 February 1883, Madan Lal was sent to England in 1906 by his father to pursue mechanical engineering. However, concerns soon arose within the family that Madan Lal was deviating from the academic path and getting involved in anti-British revolutionary activities in England. Troubled by this, Kundan Lal Dhingra, the eldest son, wrote to Sir Curzon Wyllie, who was an old acquaintance of their father, seeking his help in steering Madan Lal back to

[67] Highest authority overseeing Indian affairs in England.

his studies. Responding to this plea, on 13 April 1909, Curzon Wyllie sent a letter to Madan Lal Dhingra, inviting him to meet at his office in London. The following is the reproduction of the letter written by Curzon Wyllie to Madan Lal Dhingra:[68]

To
Madan Lal Dhingra
Engineering student
University College
Gower Street, WC

India Office
Whitehall S.W.
13th April, 1909

Dear Sir,

Your brother Mr. K.L. Dhingra, whose acquaintance I had the pleasure of making in England, has written to tell me that you are in London and asking me to be of any assistance I can to you.

I expect to be abroad from the 15th to the 30th of April, but on my return I shall be very pleased to see you at the India Office if you can conveniently call between 11 and 1 or 2:30 and 3:30.

I remain,

Your faithfully,
WHC Waylie
Lt Colonel

Madan Lal Dhingra did not respond to the letter sent by Sir Curzon Wyllie, as he firmly regarded British officers like

[68]Waraich, Malwinder Jit Singh, *Tryst with Martyrdom: Trial of Madan Lal Dhingra*, Unistar Books, Chandigarh, 2013.

Wyllie as oppressors of India, instrumental in suppressing the aspirations of Indians for independence. While Dhingra had few friends in England, he frequently visited India House, located at 65, Cromwell Avenue, Highgate, London. It was there that he first met and befriended Vinayak Damodar Savarkar. At that time, India House had become a vibrant hub for Indian nationalist students in Britain. The founder of India House was Shyamji Krishna Varma, a distinguished scholar of both Sanskrit and English. Varma had established India House to provide accommodation for Indian students who had come to England for higher education but lacked a place to stay. However, it soon evolved into much more than just a residence; it became a centre for revolutionary thought and nationalist activities. Among its most notable residents was Vinayak Damodar Savarkar, whose ideas and passion for India's liberation left a lasting impact on Dhingra.

Day of Assassination

Dhingra and his associates at India House believed that Sir William Curzon Wyllie, through his involvement with the National Indian Association, was attempting to foster loyalty towards the British Empire among Indian students. They also suspected that he monitored the activities of India House residents and regularly reported their movements to local intelligence agencies. This surveillance by Wyllie further fuelled Madan Lal Dhingra's animosity towards him. On 1 July 1909, the National Indian Association organized a social event titled 'At Home' at the Imperial Institute in South Kensington, London. The gathering was attended by a large number of Indian students and British guests.

While the Association officially claimed to support Indian

students in the UK, its covert aim was to nurture allegiance to the British Empire. Sir Curzon Wyllie, who held the position of Treasurer in the Association, arrived at the venue at around 10.30 p.m. Among the attendees was also Madan Lal Dhingra, who had accepted the invitation with an entirely different motive. Dhingra had come armed with two pistols and a dagger, intent on assassinating Curzon Wyllie.

At approximately 10.40 p.m., Dhingra engaged Curzon Wyllie in conversation near the hall's entrance. After a few minutes, he drew his pistol and fired four shots at Wyllie, which killed him on the spot. Witnessing the attack, Dr Cawas Lalcaca, a Parsi doctor, rushed to Wyllie's aid. In what he later claimed was self-defence, Dhingra fired two more shots, seriously injuring Dr Lalcaca, who succumbed to his wounds shortly thereafter. The assassination of Sir Curzon Wyllie marked the first modern political assassination on British soil and carried immense historical significance for the Indian revolutionary movement abroad. Soon after the incident, the police arrived and arrested Madan Lal Dhingra, taking him to Wacton Street Police Station. He was subsequently presented before the Westminster Police Court, where Mr Horace Smith presided as Magistrate. On 10 July 1909, Dhingra made a bold and unapologetic statement before the Magistrate, declaring:[69]

> I do not want to say anything in defence of myself, but simply to prove the justice of my deed. As for myself, no English Law Court has got any authority to arrest and detain me in prison, or pass sentence of death on

[69]'MADAR LAL DHINGRA,. Killing; murder. 19th July 1909.', *The Proceedings of the Old Bailey*, https://tinyurl.com/m79bj9xf. Accessed on 7 January 2026.

me. This is the reason I did not have any counsel to defend me.

And I maintain that if it is patriotic for an English man to fight against the German if they were to occupy this country, it is much more justifiable and patriotic in my case to fight against the English. I hold the English people responsible for the murder of 80 millions of Indian people in the last 50 years, and they are also responsible for taking away 100,000,000 pounds every year from India to this country. I also hold them responsible for the hanging and deportation of my patriotic countrymen, who did just the same as the English people here are advising their countrymen to do. And the Englishman who goes out to India and gets, say £ 100 a month, that simply means that he passes a sentence of death on a thousand of my countrymen, because these thousand people could easily live on this £ 100 which the Englishman spends mostly on his frivolities and pleasures. Just as the Germans have no right to occupy this country, so the English people have no right to occupy India, and it is perfectly justifiable on our part to kill the Englishman who is polluting our sacred land. I am surprised at the terrible hypocrisy, the farce, and the mockery of the English people. They pose as the champions of oppressed humanity, when there is terrible oppression and horrible atrocities committed In India; for example, the killing of two millions of people every year and the outraging of our women. In case this country is occupied by Germans, and the Englishman not bearing to see the Germans walking with insolence of conquerors in the streets of London, goes and kills one or two Germans, and that Englishman

> is held as a patriot by the people of this country, then certainly I am prepared to work for the emancipation of my Motherland. Whatever else I have to say is in the paper before the Court. (After Dhingra's arrest his written statement was recovered by the police, from his pocket and the police ignored his request to produce his statement in the court.) I make this statement, not because I wish to plead for mercy or anything of that kind. I wish that English people sentence me to death, for in that case the vengeance of my countrymen will be all the more keen. I put forward this statement to show the justice of my cause to the outside world, and especially to our sympathizers in America and Germany.

Madan Lal Dhingra further clarified that he had had no intention of harming Dr Cawas Lalcaca, but when the doctor had attempted to physically restrain him, he fired in self-defence. He also stated that he had no prior acquaintance with Dr Lalcaca. Throughout the trial, Dhingra chose not to engage any legal counsel. He even refused to cross-examine the witnesses presented by the prosecution. At the time of his arrest, the police recovered a written statement from Dhingra's pocket and found another copy in his residential quarters. However, both documents were sealed by court order, and their content was never officially disclosed by the police or prosecution. The sensational nature of this assassination captured global media attention. Leading newspapers across the world reported on the incident extensively. From Britain to India, there was widespread curiosity about Madan Lal Dhingra's motive behind the killing. The British authorities and police made significant efforts to suppress Dhingra's letter which was recovered from his pocket at the time of his arrest.

However, despite their attempts, a newspaper, *The Daily News*, managed to publish a copy of his statement on 12 August 1909, under the striking headline 'Challenge'. For the readers' interest, the complete text of Madan Lal Dhingra's statement is reproduced below:[70]

> I attempted to shed English blood intentionally and of purpose, as a humble protest against the inhuman transportations and hangings of Indian youth. In this attempt I consulted none but my own conscience; conspired with none but my own duty. I believe that a nation unwillingly held down by foreign bayonets is in a perpetual state of war. Since open battle is rendered impossible I attacked by surprise - since cannon could not be had I drew forth and fired a revolver. As a Hindu I feel that the slavery of my nation is an insult to my God. Her cause is the cause of freedom. Her service is the service of Sri Krishna. Neither rich nor able, a poor son like myself can offer nothing but his blood at the altar of Mother's deliverance and so I rejoice at the prospect of my martyrdom. The only lesson required in India is to learn how to die and the only way to teach it is by dying alone. The soul is immortal and if every one of my countrymen takes at least two lives of Englishmen before his body falls the Mother's salvation is a day's work. This war ceases not only with the independence of India alone, it shall continue as long as the English and Hindu races exist in this world. Until our country is free Sri Krishna stands exhorting 'if killed you attain Heaven; if successful

[70]Sareen, Tilak Raj, *Indian Revolutionary Movement Abroad, 1905–1921*, Sterling Publishers, New Delhi, 1979.

> you win the earth. It is my fervent prayer, may I be reborn of the same mother and may I re-die in the same sacred cause, till my mission is done and she stands free for the good of humanity and to the glory of God.

THE TRIAL

Madan Lal Dhingra's trial was held at the Old Bailey, officially known as the Central Criminal Court of London. The proceedings began on 23 July 1909, during which the prosecution examined several witnesses against Dhingra. However, for the readers' benefit, we present here a summary of the testimonies from only the key witnesses, who were:

Emmma Josephine Beck[71]

The Honorary Secretary of the National Indian Association, Emmma Josephine Beck, testified before the court that she had first met Madan Lal Dhingra approximately four months ago in London. She had personally sent Dhingra an invitation ticket to the 'At Home' event. She confirmed Dhingra's presence at the event, stating she first saw him shortly after 9.00 p.m., while Sir William Wyllie arrived later, around 10.30 p.m.

According to her testimony, at around 10.40 p.m., she had a brief conversation with Dhingra, who informed her that he had completed his course at University College and would appear for the M.I.C.E. examination in October. When Ms Emmma asked if he knew many people at the event, Dhingra replied that he knew only a few. The Secretary further confirmed

[71]Waraich, Malwinder Jit Singh, *Tryst with Martyrdom: Trial of Madan Lal Dhingra*, Unistar Books, Chandigarh, 2003.

Dhingra's address as 108, Ledbury Road, in her statement and stated that she had previously written to him there.

Sir Lesley Probyn[72]

A long-time acquaintance of Sir William Curzon Wyllie, Sir Lesley Probyn recalled arriving at the Imperial Institute around 10.50 p.m. on 1 July, where an event organized by the National Indian Association was underway. The gathering, held in a large hall of the institute, was attended by a significant number of English and Indian guests, including Sir Wyllie and Lady Wyllie. At approximately 11.00 p.m., as the witness and his wife approached the exit, they suddenly heard three to four gunshots fired in quick succession, followed shortly by another shot. Upon moving towards the vestibule, the witness saw the accused holding a revolver, although it was not aimed at anyone at that moment. Immediately after another shot was fired, the accused appeared to turn the weapon toward his own temple, prompting the witness to intervene. He grabbed the accused's left hand with his right, and then took control of the revolver.

During the scuffle, the witness fell and sustained some injuries but maintained his grip on both the revolver and the accused. Mr Sinha, another Indian gentleman and witness in this case, assisted in restraining Dhingra. After a brief struggle, the police arrived, and the witness identified Dhingra as the shooter. He also recalled Dhingra asking for his spectacles, which Mr Sinha helped him wear. The witness held on to the revolver throughout and later handed it over to an Inspector, confirming in court that the weapon shown was the same used in the incident.

[72]Ibid.

Madan Mohan Sinha[73]

An Indian law student at Middle Temple and a member of the National Indian Association, Madan Mohan Sinha had arrived at the event at the Imperial Institute on 1 July around 9.20 or 9.30 p.m. He personally knew Sir William Wyllie and saw him arrive at approximately 10.35 or 10.40 p.m. By 11.10 p.m., Mr Sinha was in the hall, about five or six yards from the vestibule door, with a clear line of sight. Upon hearing gunshots, he turned and saw Madan Lal Dhingra aiming and firing a revolver at Sir Curzon Wyllie from a distance of about two yards or less.

According to the witness, Dhingra appeared to shoot from behind and to the left side. He observed smoke from the shot and saw Sir Wyllie collapse near the door. As the witness rushed towards the scene, Dhingra briefly pointed the gun towards him but then turned it towards his own head (probably in an attempt to take his own life), though the gun only clicked without firing. The witness managed to grab Dhingra from behind, lift his arms and push him down over some chairs. He continued to restrain Dhingra by placing his knee on Dhingra's back, despite the accused's struggle to free himself. The witness shouted for help while maintaining his hold, until two police officers arrived. During this time, Dhingra asked for his spectacles, which had fallen off, and someone helped put them back on. The witness noticed Sir Wyllie's body lying near the door and Dr Lalcaca's body further inside only after the struggle ended. Mr Sinha also confirmed that a second revolver and a large hunting knife were recovered from Dhingra, and identified the displayed pistol as the one used in the shooting.

[73]Ibid.

Captain Douglas W. Thornburn[74]

Captain Douglas W. Thornburn was present at the Imperial Institute on 1 July, having arrived at around 9.00 p.m. According to his testimony, at approximately 11.00 p.m., while near the Reception Hall doors, he looked into the vestibule and saw two men conversing at arm's length. They would later be identified as Sir Curzon Wyllie and Madan Lal Dhingra, who was dressed in a lounge suit and blue turban.

Almost immediately, Mr Thornburn witnessed Dhingra raise his arm and fire four rapid shots directly at Sir Curzon Wyllie's face. The shots were fired in such quick succession that Wyllie collapsed only after the fourth shot. A few seconds later, two additional shots were fired, though the witness couldn't tell the direction of the revolver.

As per the statement of Mr Thornburn, when he rushed toward Dhingra, he noticed someone had fallen near the staircase, likely Dr Cawas Lalcaca. Dhingra then attempted to shoot himself, placing the revolver to his right temple, but the gun only produced a click. He was immediately seized by others, including the witness, who asked, 'Why have you done this?', but Dhingra remained silent, only mentioning something about his spectacles. The journalist then saw the bodies of Sir Curzon Wyllie and Dr Lalcaca on the floor, noting that Dr Lalcaca was still alive at that time.

Captain Charles Rolleston[75]

Captain Charles Rolleston was a retired army officer and he testified before the court that he was present as a guest at

[74]Ibid.

[75]Ibid.

the 'At Home' event held at the Imperial Institute on 1 July. Around 10.45 to 11.00 p.m., while in the hall, he heard five gunshots in quick succession. Looking towards the vestibule, he saw a cloud of smoke and a young man in a lounge suit and blue turban emerge, raise a revolver in his right hand, take deliberate aim at an Indian gentleman in European dress and fire a shot from a distance of about five or six feet. The Indian gentleman fell instantly. As the officer moved into the vestibule, he saw Sir Curzon Wyllie's body lying in a pool of blood. About three to four yards away was the body of the Indian gentleman, who would later be identified as Dr Cawas Lalcaca, writhing in pain on the ground. The assailant, Madan Lal Dhingra, was already being restrained by two or three men.

The witness saw a revolver and a dagger being taken from Dhingra. He personally searched Dhingra's inner pocket, recovering several items including a folded foolscap paper, other small documents, a pen knife (6–7 inches), keys, a spectacle case, gloves and a handkerchief. All items were handed over to the police. He questioned Dhingra in English, asking for his name and address. Dhingra told him his name and that he lived at Ledbury Road. When asked about his motive, Dhingra simply said, 'I'll tell the police.' The officer then tried speaking to him in Hindustani, but Dhingra did not respond. The witness informed the court that this interaction occurred before the police arrived.

Judgment Day

The trial was notably brief, largely due to the absence of any defence counsel and the lack of cross-examination by the accused. Madan Lal Dhingra, even though he was entitled to question the witnesses, chose not to exercise that right. After each witness concluded their testimony, Chief Justice Lord Alverstone of Old Bailey would turn to the dock and ask, 'Mr Dhingra, do you wish to question the witness?' To which Dhingra would respond with a 'no' each time.

Finally, on 23 July 1909, after the prosecution had concluded its examination of all the witnesses, the Lord Chief Justice turned to Madan Lal Dhingra again. He again asked him whether he wished to summon any witness or present anything in his defence. Dhingra calmly replied that he wished to read his statement which he had earlier given before the Magistrate and beyond it he had nothing further to add. He said that he accepted all charges brought against him. The Chief Justice, visibly perturbed by Dhingra's unflinching admission and lack of resistance, warned him that political speeches would not be tolerated in court.

If Dhingra had anything to say, it would have to be relevant to the case and the court would not hear any criticism of British rule in India. To this, Dhingra replied firmly that if he would not be allowed to read his statement then he had nothing further to offer in his defence. The court was free to impose whatever punishment it thought appropriate. The Chief Justice was in no mood to hear the political speeches of Dhingra, so he indicated to his clerk to read the verdict. The clerk of the court immediately stood up and read the verdict handed over to him by the jury: 'Madan Lal Dhingra, you are found guilty of the wilful murder of Sir William Curzon Wyllie.'

After delivering the verdict, the Judge Lord Alverstone asked Dhingra to state the reason why the maximum penalty (capital punishment) should not be imposed on him. Dhingra's response rang through the courtroom with defiance. He said:[76]

> I have told you over and over again that I do not acknowledge the authority of the Court. You can do whatever you like. I do not mind at all. You can pass sentence of death on me. I do not care. You white people are all powerful now, but remember, we shall have our turn in the time to come, when we can do what we like.

Moved by Madan Lal Dhingra's defiant stance, the Chief Justice promptly pronounced the sentence of death. Addressing the accused, he declared, 'Mr. Madan Lal Dhingra, you shall be hanged by the neck until you are dead.' Hearing this, bailiffs present in the court approached Dhingra to escort him out of the courtroom. Dhingra immediately turned to the judge, with a proud smile on his face, and said: 'Thank you, my Lord. I don't care. I am proud to have the honour of laying down my life for the cause of my motherland.'[77]

Interestingly, as the judge was about to sign the death warrant, Mr Tindal Atkinson, a senior counsel, appeared on behalf of Dhingra's family. Under the instruction of his client, he submitted to the court that the accused's actions had brought shame upon the entire Dhingra family, and after the incident they had severed all ties with him. He further submitted, particularly on behalf of Dhingra's father, that no family could be more loyal to the British Crown than theirs. Hearing Mr Tindal Atkinson, the Chief Justice responded:[78]

---

[76]'MADAR LAL DHINGRA,. Killing; murder. 19th July 1909.', *The Proceedings of the Old Bailey*, https://tinyurl.com/m79bj9xf. Accessed on 7 January 2026.
[77]Ibid.
[78]Ibid.

> Mr. Tindal Atkinson, although the course may have seemed somewhat unusual, having regard to the nature of this crime and the wicked attempts at justification in some quarters, I am very glad you should have said that on behalf of the members of the family.

With that, the judge snapped the nib of his pen after signing the death warrant, symbolically severing the final bond between the court and the condemned. He then withdrew silently into his chamber.

Aftermath

Madan Lal Dhingra was executed on 17 August 1909 at Pentonville Jail in England, becoming the first Indian to be hanged on British soil for the cause of India's freedom. When his comrades from India House requested the return of his body for cremation, the British jail authorities denied the request. His mortal remains were quietly buried in a secluded corner of the prison ground. After Dhingra went to the gallows, *The Times*, London, wrote an editorial titled 'Conviction of Dhingra'. The editorial said, 'The nonchalance displayed by the assassin was of a character which is happily unusual in such trials in this country. He asked no questions. He maintained a defiance of studied indifference. He walked smiling from the dock.'[79] Churchill also reluctantly admitted that Dhingra's last words in court were the finest ever made in the name of patriotism.[80]

---

[79]Kaur, Jasneet, 'A Forgotten Martyr-Madan Lal Dhingra', *Purva Mimaansa*, Vol. 7, No. 1, March-September 2016, pp. 1–6.

[80]Sareen, Tilak Raj, *Indian Revolutionary Movement Abroad*, 1905–1921, Sterling Publishers, New Delhi, 1979.

Although Dhingra's ultimate sacrifice went on to inspire future revolutionaries like Bhagat Singh and Udham Singh, his own family chose to disown him permanently in an effort to demonstrate their allegiance to the British Empire. Decades later, in a symbolic act of honour and remembrance, the Government of India repatriated his remains on 13 December 1976. His ashes were finally consigned to flames with full Hindu rites on Indian soil, bringing home a hero whose courage had long transcended borders.

ELEVEN

TRIAL OF UDHAM SINGH

'Your action is correct. Lieutenant Governor approves.'

—Sir Michael Francis O'Dwyer,
Lieutenant Governor of Punjab

When Colonel Reginald Dyer received this short telegram from Lieutenant Governor Sir Michael Francis O'Dwyer, approving his action in Jallianwala Bagh, he felt relieved and showed no remorse for his brutal act of ordering the massacre of hundreds of unarmed civilians gathered at Jallianwala Bagh in Amritsar on 13 April 1919. Following Gandhi's call to protest against the Rowlatt Act,[81] anti-British demonstrations in Punjab intensified, prompting the imposition of martial law. As the administrator of Punjab, Sir Michael O'Dwyer believed that Punjab was on the edge of an uprising akin to the 1857 revolt. Concerned about losing control over the province, he granted Colonel Dyer unrestricted authority to act, thereby making himself complicit in the Jallianwala Bagh Massacre. Among those deeply scarred by the massacre was 20-year-old Udham Singh. The tragic incident, which claimed the lives of

[81]Rowlatt Act was a law passed in 1919 by the British Government severely curtailing the few existing civil liberties of Indians.

many of his friends, ignited a lifelong hatred in him for British rule in India. Orphaned at the age of seven, Udham Singh was brought up in an orphanage and grew into a solitary young man. He eventually became involved with revolutionary circles and formed friendships with individuals like Bhagat Singh. In 1931, after being imprisoned for possessing unlicensed firearms, he was released and later travelled to England under a different identity. There, he began to meticulously plan the assassination of Sir Michael O'Dwyer to avenge the horrors of Jallianwala Bagh.

Finally, Udham Singh got the opportunity to kill Michael O'Dwyer on 13 March 1940, when the East India Association and the Royal Central Asian Society hosted a lecture on Afghanistan at Caxton Hall in London. The event started at 3 p.m. and drew a large audience (almost 450 people) and featured several prominent figures, like Sir Michael O'Dwyer, Brigadier General Sir Percy Sykes, Sir Louis Dane (former Lieutenant Governor of Punjab), Lord Zetland (former Secretary of State for India), and Lord Lamington (former Governor of Bombay). As the lecture concluded and attendees began to disperse, Udham Singh emerged from the crowd, drew his revolver and fired three shots, killing Sir Michael O'Dwyer on the spot. Udham Singh also fired at Lord Zetland, Sir Louis Dane and Lord Lamington. Although they were slightly injured, they survived.

Initially, most people thought this attack was the work of the Irish Republican Army (IRA). That was until Udham Singh was arrested. Udham Singh was apprehended by members of the public present in the hall and handed over to the police. He was subsequently placed in the custody of Detective Sergeant Sidney Jones who then took him to Cannon Row

Police Station in London. Initially, Udham Singh identified himself as Mohammad Singh Azad, but after investigation, the police discovered his true identity. During his interrogation at the police station, Udham Singh calmly stated, 'I did it because I held a grudge against him. He deserved it.' When Detective Sidney Jones warned him that he might face the death penalty for the murder of Sir Michael O'Dwyer, Singh remained unfazed. With unwavering resolve, he declared, 'I don't care about the sentence of death. It doesn't worry me. I am dying for a purpose.'[82]

The assassination of a former high-ranking British official caused a major stir across London and beyond. Newspapers around the world closely followed the case, publishing even the smallest details about Udham Singh and the killing of Sir Michael O'Dwyer. When the news reached India, it was met with mixed emotions. For many, it felt as if justice had finally been delivered, even if it had come after the long wait of 21 years. Udham Singh's act was hailed as a powerful retaliation for the Jallianwala Bagh Massacre, and he was revered as a hero for avenging the bloodshed of 1919.

Udham Singh's trial commenced on 4 June 1940 at the Central Criminal Court (Old Bailey) before Justice Atkinson. The prosecution, led by senior Treasury Counsel Mr G.B. McClure, presented several prominent witnesses who testified against the accused. Udham Singh was represented by Mr John Hutchinson and Mr V.K. Krishna Menon. Although Singh was initially prepared to accept all the charges pressed against him

---

[82]Roychowdhury, Adrija, 'Udham Singh, the Witness to Jallianwala Bagh, Who Swore to Bring an End to British Rule', *The Indian Express*, 14 October 2021, https://tinyurl.com/42ud2hy2. Accessed on 6 January 2025.

and refused to present any defence, his legal team persuaded him to adopt their version of events. Udham Singh's counsels claimed in court that he had not intended to kill O'Dwyer and had carried the revolver only as a symbolic act of protest. The defence maintained its stand in the entire trial that the shooting was unintentional.

However, given the political shock and the sort of sensation this assassination had created among the British public, it was certain from the beginning that a death sentence was inevitable. The trial lasted just two days. On 5 June 1940, the court sentenced Udham Singh to death. The 12-member jury returned a unanimous guilty verdict within an hour and a half, convicting Udham Singh for the murder of Sir Michael O'Dwyer.

THE TRIAL

The King v. Udham Singh
Central Criminal Court (Old Bailey)
04 June 1940–6 June 1940

As previously mentioned, several eyewitnesses who were present at Caxton Hall during the assassination of Sir Michael O'Dwyer testified against Udham Singh in court. While it is not feasible to include the testimonies of all witnesses here, below is a summary of the accounts of two notable individuals, Bertha Herring and Claud Wyndham Hurry Riches, who claimed to have apprehended Udham Singh after the incident:

Testimony of Miss Bertha Herring [83]

Bertha Herring testified before the court that she had attended the lecture at Caxton Hall on 13 March 1940. Arriving around 2.55 p.m., she had sat on the right side of the hall in the fourth row. She observed the accused, Udham Singh, standing about five yards away, near the right-hand gangway, leaning against the wall. When the meeting ended, and the witness bent to collect her belongings, she heard a gunshot followed by two more. Looking up, she saw a revolver in Singh's hand and saw flashes from the shots. She believed Sir Michael O'Dwyer was in front, but couldn't see exactly how close Singh was to him when the shots were fired.

Miss Bertha Herring shouted for people to catch Singh. As Singh moved towards the front, she ran to stop him, grabbing his shoulder. Singh resisted and threw her back, but she managed to catch his coat lapel, and they fell together onto chairs before others restrained Singh. She further testified that afterwards she saw Sir Michael O'Dwyer lying fatally wounded on the ground and Lord Lamington bleeding from his wrist.

Testimony of Claud Wyndham Hurry Riches[84]

According to the testimony of Mr Riches, a retired general manager, he was present at the Tudor Room, Caxton Hall, on the afternoon of 13 March 1940 when the murder of Mr Michael O'Dwyer took place. He was seated in the fifth or sixth row from the front, on the right-hand side, with one chair separating him from the gangway. He noticed Udham

[83]National Archives of India, 'Trial of Udham Singh-File No. ACC 699', *Abhilekh-Patal*. Accessed on 7 January 2026.
[84]Ibid.

Singh during the lecture, standing against the wall to his right, somewhere midway between his seat and the front row. At the end of the meeting, he saw Singh move towards the dais, but then lost sight of him. Suddenly, a flash and a loud bang went off, followed by approximately four more shots, seemingly coming from the area in front of the first row. Mr Riches further testified that amid the resulting confusion and pushing, he saw Singh nearby, holding a revolver at waist level.

Acting quickly, he stepped into the gangway, turned and leapt onto Singh's back, striking at his right arm. Singh's movements had already slowed, possibly due to someone else intervening. Both men crashed to the ground, and Mr Riches managed to grab Singh's right wrist, causing him to drop the revolver, which was then recovered by Major Slee. Mr Riches confirmed that Singh lay on the ground and was subdued by others until the police arrived. After the shooting, he saw Sir Michael O'Dwyer lying dead and Lord Zetland, Sir Louis Dane and Lord Lamington lying injured and receiving first aid.

Statement of Udham Singh

Once all the prosecution witnesses had testified, the court invited the accused, Udham Singh, to make a statement or say something in his defence. As previously mentioned, Udham Singh initially intended to plead guilty. However, on the advice of his legal team, he changed his stance in court and claimed that he had fired at the wall and that the bullet accidentally struck Sir Michael O'Dwyer and the others. He asserted that his intention was merely to stage a protest and not to kill anyone. Interestingly, before giving his statement in court, he refused to take an oath on the Bible and instead chose to make a solemn affirmation. Here is the exact reproduction of Udham Singh's statement as recorded in court:[85]

> Yesterday about half past 11 to 12, I went to the India Office to see someone, Sir Hussan Suhrawardy. The fellow on the gate he told me he was out. He told me I could wait for him if I wanted. I went in the waiting room, but I was coming out I saw a notice about a meeting will be held at Caxton Hall. I came out and the fellow on the door said I could see Sir Hussan at, I think, a quarter to 4. I walked out and I did not go back. I thought to see him this morning so he could help me for to get the endorsement to the passport. This morning I got up to see Sir Hussan, but I changed my mind. I thought he would not be able to help me. When I left home this morning I thought I would see the Paul Robeson picture in the Leicester Square. I want there and it was not open yet. I went back home again. Then I thought it was time to go to this afternoon meeting to protest. I take my revolver from home with me to protest. In the beginning of the meeting I was standing up. I did not take the revolver to kill, but just to protest. Well, them [sic] when the meeting was already finished I took the revolver from my pocket and I shoot like I think at the wall. I just shot just to make the protest. I have seen people starving in India under British Imperialism. I have done it: the pistol went off three or four times. I am not sorry for protesting. It was my duty to do so. Put some more. Just for the sake of my country to protest. I do not mind what sentence. 10, 20 or 50 years or

[85]Ibid.

to be hanged. I have done my duty. Actually I did not mean to take a person's life, do you understand? I just mean protesting, you know. I have read this statement and it is true.

Judgment Day (5 June 1940)

Once all the witnesses and the accused had finished recording their statements before the court and the jury, the clerk of the court, on the indication of Justice Atkinson, stood up and asked the jury whether they had reached a verdict. In response, the foreman of the jury confirmed that they had unanimously found Udham Singh guilty of murder. Following this, the clerk asked Udham Singh if he had anything to say as to why the maximum punishment (death sentence) prescribed by law should not be imposed. Udham Singh replied that he had a statement to make and wished for the jury to hear it. As soon as Udham Singh started reading his statement, Justice Atkinson immediately intervened, warning that no political speech would be tolerated, and that Udham Singh could only speak on matters directly relevant to the case. Udham Singh continued his speech, which passionately criticized the British government, holding them responsible for his country's dire situation and condemning their exploitative policies towards India, put in place for their own gain.

At that point, Mr McClure, the counsel for the prosecution, stood and reminded the judge that under the wartime emergency powers, the court could prohibit publication of such statements. Responding swiftly, Justice Atkinson directed the press who were taking notes in the courtroom that nothing that Udham Singh had said was to be published. Meanwhile, Singh continued reading from his note. Justice Atkinson then asked Singh to hand over his written statement so it could be shared with the jury. Singh refused, insisting that he wanted to read it aloud himself. Once again, the judge reminded him that he was only permitted to speak on matters related to the case and not on political issues or the governance of India. Udham Singh persisted and continued with his statement.

Below is the verbatim transcript of the exchange that took place between Justice Atkinson and Udham Singh immediately before the court pronounced the death sentence on him:[86]

Udham Singh: I do not care about dying. That is not worrying me. I am dying for others, you see. May I still read it?

Justice Atkinson: Say anything you have got to say to the point, but as far as I could hear you, you began by denouncing the British government or the British Empire, and we are not going to have that here. That is nothing to the point.

Udham Singh: I am not afraid to die. I am proud to die. I want to help my native land, and I hope when I have gone that in my place will come others of my countrymen to drive the dirty dogs, when I am free of the country. I am standing before an English Jury in an English Court. You people go to India and when you come back you are given prizes and put into the House of Commons, but when we come to England we are put to death. In any case I do not care anything about it, but when you dirty dogs come to India, the Intellectuals they call themselves, the rulers- they are a bastard blood caste, and they order machine guns to fire on the Indian students without hesitation. I have nothing against the public at all. I have more English friends in England than I have in India. I have nothing

[86]Ibid.

against the public. I have great sympathy with the workers of England, but I am against the dirty British Government. Your people are suffering the same as I am suffering through those dirty dogs and mad beasts-killing, mutilating and destroying. We know what is going on in India hundreds of thousands of people being killed by your dirty dogs.

Justice Atkinson: I am not going to hear any more of this, so you can put this paper away. I am going to pass sentence upon you.

Udham Singh: You do not want to hear this anymore. I have to say a lot.

Judge: I am not going to hear any more of that but if you have anything relevant to say.

Udham Singh: You asked me if I had anything to say.

Judge: I am not going to hear any more of that.

Udham Singh: You people are dirty. You don't want to hear from us what you are doing in India. Beasts, beasts, beasts. England, down with imperialism, down with the dirty dogs.

Frustration was visible on Justice Atkinson's face as Udham Singh's unwavering defiance echoed through the courtroom. The accused refused to be silenced, refused to conform and refused to beg. Now Justice Atkinson was no longer willing to entertain the speech of Udham Singh and brought the moment to its grim end. Without another word, he delivered the final blow, the sentence of death, the maximum punishment allowed under the law for murder. Before the silence could settle, Mr McClure rose once more. He gently reminded the judge that a formal order should be passed barring the press from publishing any part of Udham Singh's courtroom remarks. Judge Atkinson nodded in agreement. Turning to the reporters, he made it clear: 'Nothing said by the accused in this court shall be published.'

Justice Atkinson then quietly retired to his chamber, while Udham Singh was escorted to Pentonville Jail in London, where he was placed in solitary confinement.

Aftermath

Udham Singh did not file an appeal against the verdict sentencing him to death. Therefore, on 31 July 1940, he was executed at Pentonville Prison, London. His final statement in court, along with other significant information about him, was heavily censored and confined to official records. The British authorities were deeply concerned that Udham Singh might use the courtroom as a political platform to present himself as a martyr, thereby motivating Indians both within India and abroad to commit similar acts.

Therefore, the British government both in England and India prohibited the press from glorifying Singh, fearing that his legacy might inspire others to follow the path of revolution. Regrettably, prominent leaders such as Mahatma Gandhi and Pandit Nehru were critical of Singh's act of retribution. Gandhi, expressing his disapproval, remarked:[87]

> The news of the death of Michael O'Dwyer and the injuries to Lord Zetland, Lord Lamington and Sir Louis

---

[87]Roychowdhury, Adrija, 'Udham Singh, the Witness to Jallianwala Bagh, Who Swore to Bring an End to British Rule', *The Indian Express*, 14 October 2021, https://tinyurl.com/42ud2hy2. Accessed on 6 January 2026.

> Dane has caused me deep pain. I regard this act as one of insanity.' Gandhi further said that he hoped that the incident would not impact Indian politics and also extended his condolences to O' Dwyer's family.

After independence, thanks to the efforts of various sections of society, Udham Singh's legacy continues to thrive in multiple forms—through memorials built in his honour, museums that safeguard his story and the naming of a district in Uttarakhand as Udham Singh Nagar. Sardar Udham Singh will always remain an enduring symbol of resistance, inspiring generations with his courage and his ultimate sacrifice for the cause of a free India.

TWELVE

TRIAL OF MANGAL PANDEY

Mangal Pandey is regarded as one of the first revolutionaries of India, as he was the earliest to raise his voice against the mighty British Empire. At just 26 years old, he defied orders from his senior army officers who commanded him to use cartridges greased with cow and pig fat. Born in Ballia, Uttar Pradesh, Mangal Pandey joined the 5th Company of the 34th Bengal Native Infantry at the age of 19. Deeply devoted to his religion, he served the Company obediently for seven years.

However, in 1857 when news spread in Barrackpore (West Bengal), where his company was posted, that the cartridges that the army were using were coated with cow and pig fat, many native soldiers grew agitated, viewing this as an attempt by the British to convert them to Christianity. This fear also intensified after the introduction of the Hindu Widows' Remarriage Act, which permitted IIindu widows to remarry. There was widespread belief among the Indian population, especially the native soldiers, that the British were deliberately targeting their religious beliefs and actively promoting Christian missionaries to convert native Indians.

It would be incorrect to claim that the British were unaware of the growing discontent among the native soldiers. Major-General J.B. Hearsey, who was in command of the Presidency Division (which included the Barrackpore cantonment), made sincere efforts to dispel the confusion surrounding the cartridges. However, his attempts had little impact.

On the afternoon of 29 March 1857, an angry Mangal Pandey, dressed in his regimental uniform and a dhoti, came out to the parade ground. He tried to encourage other soldiers to join him in rebellion. When senior officers like Lieutenant B.H. Baugh and Sergeant-Major J.T. Hewson heard about the incident, they rushed to the parade ground to arrest Sepoy Mangal Pandey. Seeing them approach, Mangal Pandey fired from his gun, targeting Lieutenant Baugh. Lieutenant B.H. Baugh narrowly escaped, but his horse was killed. A sword fight broke out between Pandey and the officers. Both Baugh and Hewson were badly injured in the fight, but managed to escape when another native sepoy, Shaikh Paltu, grabbed Mangal Pandey from behind. Realizing he would be captured, Mangal Pandey shot himself with his musket[88] and was severely wounded.

The British feared that the rebellion might spread among other soldiers, so they quickly set up a 14-member court of inquiry. Mangal Pandey was charged with inciting mutiny and using violence against officers. On 8 April 1857, Mangal Pandey was hanged as punishment. His trial lasted only three days. Even though he was seriously injured, he was still cross-examined just to complete legal formalities. The British did not want him to be seen as a martyr, so they ended the process quickly without waiting for him to recover. After the trial, Shaikh Paltu was promoted for saving the lives of the British officers. As a collective punishment, the British disbanded the

---

[88]A musket gun is an early variety of firearm that was widely used by infantry soldiers in the 19th century.

entire 34th Bengal Native Infantry regiment.

The trial or court-martial of Mangal Pandey took place on 5–7 April 1857. The President of the Court was Subadar-Major Jawahar Lal Tiwari of the 43rd Regiment, Native Infantry. The following individuals served as members of this court.

Subadar	BHOLA OPUDEAH
Subadar	HURRUCK SING
Subadar	RAM SING
Subadar	LALLA RAM BUKSH
Subadar	SEWUMBUR PANDY
Subadar	DIRGA RAM
Subadar	MEERWAN SING
Subadar	KHOODA BUKSH
Subadar	SOOKHLAL MISR
Subadar	AJOODHIA TEWARY
Subadar	JALIM SING
Subadar	DEWAN ALLIE
Subadar	MOHUN SING
Subadar	AMANUT KHAN

Judge Advocate: Captain G.C. Hatch, Deputy Judge Advocate-General, Presidency Division.

Interpeter: Lieutenant James Vallings, 19" Regiment, Native Infantry.

The court convened at 11 a.m. on 5 April 1857 at the Mess House of the 34th Regiment of Native Infantry in Barrackpore. President, Members, Judge Advocate, and Interpreter all were present. Sepoy Mangal Pandey, No. 1446, of the 5th Company,

34th Regiment, Native Infantry, was brought in to court as a prisoner. The names of the president and members of the court were read aloud to him. When asked by the judge advocate whether he had any objection to being tried by the president or any member of the court-martial, Mangal Pandey responded that he had no objection. Following this, the charges against him, ordered by Major-General J. B. Hearsey, Commander of the Presidency Division, were formally read out.

Charge 1: Mutiny

The accused, Mangal Pandey, on 29 March 1857, appeared on the parade ground in front of his regiment's quarter-guard,[89] armed with a sword and a musket. There, he used language intended to provoke the soldiers of his regiment to rise up and join him in defying the lawful authority of the British Army.

Charge 2: Assault on Superior Officers

On the same occasion described above, Mangal Pandey used violence against his superior officers, namely Sergeant-Major James Thornton Hewson and Lieutenant Henry Baugh of the 34th Native Infantry. He fired his loaded musket at each of them and then proceeded to strike and injure them with his sword.

The judge advocate then asked Sepoy Mangal Pandey whether he would plead guilty to the charge. Mangal Pandey replied, 'Not guilty.' After that, the handcuffs were removed from the prisoner. The following five witnesses were called by the prosecution to make the case against Mangal Pandey.

1. Colonel S.G. Wheler

---

[89]Quarter guard is a small, armed detachment of soldiers stationed at the entrance of a military unit's base or camp.

2. Sergeant-Major J.T. Hewson
3. Lieutenant B.H. Baugh
4. Drummer John Lewis
5. Havildar Shaik Pultoo

Below is a summary of the statements given by all five witnesses:

First Witness: Colonel S.G. Wheler[90]

Colonel S.G. Wheler, who commanded the 34th Regiment, Native Infantry, was the first witness called by the prosecution. He confirmed that he commanded the 34th Regiment in his testimony. Narrating the incident of 29 March 1857 to the court, he said that on that particular day he had been informed by Captain C.C. Drury that a sepoy, Mangal Pandey, was inciting other soldiers to revolt. Wheler immediately proceeded to the parade ground where he saw Mangal Pandey, armed with a musket and a sword, walking in front of the quarter-guard. Concerned for his safety after being warned by soldiers that he could be shot, Colonel Wheler approached the quarter-guard from behind the bells-of-arms. He learnt that Lieutenant Baugh and Sergeant-Major Hewson had been wounded by Pandey. He then ordered a few men from the guard to load their weapons and instructed the native Indian officer in command to arrest Pandey.

However, the officer hesitated, saying the men were unwilling to act. Despite repeated orders, the guard only advanced a few steps before halting again. Wheler then reported the situation to the brigadier. Soon after, the major-general

[90]National Archives of India, 'Trial Proceedings of Shaheed Mangal Pandey-File No. ACC No. 342A', *Abhilekh-Patal.* Accessed on 7 January 2026.

arrived and ordered the guard forward. As they moved, Mangal Pandey shot himself. When asked about what Pandey was doing during the incident, Wheler said he was walking up and down the parade ground but he couldn't make out what Pandey was saying. He did not see the sergeant-major or the adjutant during the events. Wheler also mentioned that since late January there had been widespread talk or rumours among sepoys about the new cartridges and a belief that they were being forcibly converted to Christianity by the British missionaries. Sepoys believed that by compelling them to use cartridges greased with cow and pig fat, the British intended to undermine and destroy their religious faith. In response to this widespread rumour among the sepoys, a general parade was held on 9 February 1857 during which Major-General J.B. Hearsey (who was commanding the Presidency Division) addressed all troops on this issue to clarify the matter. After the testimony of Colonel S.G. Wheler was recorded, the court asked Mangal Pandey if he wished to cross-examine the witness. Mangal Pandey declined.

Second Witness: Sergeant-Major J.T. Hewson[91]

On the afternoon of 29 March, Hewson was informed by Naik Imam Khan that Sepoy Mangal Pandey, apparently intoxicated with bhang, was armed with a loaded musket and behaving aggressively in front of the quarter-guard. Hewson instructed Imam Khan to inform the adjutant and proceeded in full uniform to the parade ground. As he came near to the bells-of-arms, a sepoy in partial uniform (identified as Mangal Pandey) fired at him but missed. Hewson moved towards

[91]Ibid.

the quarter-guard and instructed Jemadar Ishwaree Pandy to arrest Pandey. The jemadar refused, citing the absence of Naik and Havildar, and failed to discipline or command the guard to act. Hewson tried to take control by posting sentries and observed Jemadar Ganesh Lalla talking to Mangal Pandey, apparently trying to disarm him.

Soon after, Lieutenant Baugh, the adjutant, arrived on horseback. As Baugh approached, Hewson warned him to avoid the line of fire. Pandey shot Baugh's horse; his horse died immediately and Baugh fell down. Both Baugh and Hewson advanced to confront Mangal Pandey. A violent struggle followed: Pandey attacked both with a *talwar* (sword), injuring Baugh and wounding Hewson twice. Hewson was also attacked from behind by other sepoys, believed to be from the quarter-guard. Despite being wounded and knocked down twice, Hewson tried to subdue Mangal Pandey. He later saw sepoys watching from nearby but not intervening. Hewson criticized Jemadar Ishwaree Pandy for his inaction and attempted to place him under arrest. He then retreated to his bungalow, aided by his wife and stepdaughter, and later reunited with the injured Lieutenant Baugh. When asked, Sergeant-Major J.T. Hewson confirmed hearing Mangal Pandey shout to the soldiers: '*Nikal ao, paltun*; *nikal ao hamara sath*' (Come out, men; come out and join me.)

Despite being surrounded by other sepoys, none assisted Hewson or Baugh. Hewson ended his statement by confirming he was still suffering from two sword wounds on his head. Due to his weakened state, the court did not press further questions. Mangal Pandey again declined to cross-examine the witness.

Third Witness: Lieutenant Bempde Henry Baugh[92]

Lieutenant Baugh confirmed his identity and recounted the events of 29 March. Around 5 p.m., he was informed by the Havildar-Major that Sepoy Mangal Pandey of No. 5 Company had appeared in front of the regimental quarter-guard and fired at the sergeant-major. Baugh immediately reported the incident to Colonel Wheler, armed himself, and rode swiftly to the scene. As he arrived, a gunshot was fired at him and his horse was hit and collapsed. After freeing himself, he saw Mangal Pandey reloading his weapon. Baugh fired at him, causing Pandey to stop reloading. Baugh then drew his sword and approached Pandey to arrest him. As he advanced, Pandey drew a talwar (sword). Baugh intended to retrieve another pistol but found his horse gone, so he continued to move forward and engaged Pandey in a close fight.

During the fight, which lasted five to eight minutes, Baugh sustained serious injuries; his left hand was rendered useless, and he also suffered a deep neck wound and a head injury (possibly from a musket butt). A shot was then fired from the direction of the quarter-guard, and feeling surrounded, Baugh began retreating. Throughout the fight, no one from the quarter-guard or lines helped him except for one sepoy, Shaik Pultoo of the Grenadier Company, who held Mangal Pandey from behind and allowed Baugh to retreat. Lieutenant Henry Baugh then made his way to the 43rd Regiment's sergeant-major's bungalow and was later taken to Dr Allen for medical treatment. Baugh confirmed the conflict took place approximately 40–50 paces from the quarter-guard and that his horse had been shot around eight to nine paces from it.

---

[92]Sarup, Leela, *The Trial of Mangal Pandey*, Niyogi Books, New Delhi, 2007.

He identified Mangal Pandey as the attacker and affirmed receiving the neck wound from him. During the fight, Baugh was too occupied to notice whether others present were in uniform, and he did not recall Pandey saying anything. Mangal Pandey again declined to cross-examine him.

Fourth Witness: Drummer John Lewis

Drummer John Lewis of the 34th Native Infantry testified before the court that he was on guard duty at the quarter-guard on the day of the event. In the afternoon, Mangal Pandey approached the quarter-guard shouting and asked for the bugler. Upon spotting Lewis, he ordered him to sound the assembly call. Out of fear, Lewis did not obey. Pandey then pointed his musket at him and, failing to get a response, turned to another sepoy and asked why he wasn't preparing and joining him. According to Lewis, Pandey said to the native soldiers standing there, 'It is for our religion.' He continued shouting, 'Sound the assembly.' Later, the sergeant-major approached from the left wing, and Lewis saw Pandey fire at him, though he couldn't tell where the bullet struck.

About 15 minutes later, the adjutant (Lieutenant Baugh) arrived. Pandey fired at him as well, hitting and bringing down his horse. The adjutant, armed with a pistol, continued towards Pandey on foot, joined by the sergeant-major. Pandey fired again and then attacked both officers with a sword. When asked about the actions of the jemadar (officer in charge) of the guard, Lewis stated that the jemadar did nothing and stood idly among his men during the entire incident. Lewis confirmed he did not assist nor did he see any guard members move in to help. He specifically mentioned that the jemadar or the guard did not take any action to stop the conflict.

Mangal Pandey again declined to cross-examine the witness.

Fifth Witness: Havildar Shaik Pultoo[93]

Havildar Shaik Pultoo testified before the court that on the afternoon of 29 March, he, then a sepoy (now promoted to havildar), was returning from relieving himself and saw Mangal Pandey armed, dressed in uniform and behaving aggressively. Pandey was shouting abuses and urging fellow sepoys to rise, claiming that biting cartridges would make them infidels. He shouted, 'Come out, you *bhainchute*s, the Europeans are here!', and called everyone to get ready. Seeing this, Pultoo ordered the bugler to sound the assembly, but the drummers hid. The sergeant-major soon arrived, and Mangal Pandey fired at him.

Pandey was pacing near the quarter-guard when the adjutant (Lieutenant Baugh) arrived. Pandey took aim and shot the adjutant's horse in the thigh. The horse collapsed. The adjutant drew a pistol and asked Pultoo to assist him, saying no one else was helping.

Pultoo, along with the adjutant and sergeant-major, approached Pandey. Pandey struck and wounded the adjutant with a sword on the hand, then hit the sergeant-major on the head. Pultoo tried to restrain Pandey by grabbing his waist from behind but was wounded in the hand during the struggle. As the officers retreated, some sepoys in uniform from the quarter-guard attacked the adjutant and sergeant-major with the butts of their muskets. Pultoo saw four sepoys in uniform involved but couldn't identify them as he was about 20 paces away. While the fight continued, another shot was fired from

[93]Ibid.

behind him, coming from the direction of the quarter-guard. The bullet narrowly missed the officers. When asked if Pandey was intoxicated, Pultoo said Pandey used to consume bhang, though he couldn't confirm if he had consumed it that day.

Pultoo held on to Pandey as the officers retreated and called out to the jemadar, who was nearby, to send four sepoys to help. The jemadar did not respond or send assistance. Eventually, due to his own injuries, Pultoo had to let Pandey go. Some sepoys from the quarter-guard, whose names he did not know, told him to release Pandey and interfered, urging him to let Pandey go.

After the prosecution closed its case, Mangal Pandey was called upon to present his defence. He responded, 'I did not know whom I wounded and whom I did not; what more can I say? I have nothing further to add.' When asked whether he had any evidence in his defence, he replied, 'I have no evidence.'

On that point, the court closed the defence's evidence.

Judgment Day

On 7 April 1857, the court found the prisoner, Mangal Pandey, Sepoy No. 1446 of the 5th Company, 34th Regiment, Native Infantry, guilty on both charges preferred against him. The court reassembled in the evening and the prisoner being brought before it, the court pronounced a sentence of death, namely, that he be hanged by the neck until he be dead.

Aftermath

Next day on 8 April 1857, at 5.30 a.m., Mangal Pandey was executed on the Brigade Parade Ground before the assembled troops. Alongside him, Jemadar Ishwaree Pandey of the same regiment was also sentenced to death. Ishwaree Pandey was held responsible for failing to support his senior officers during their confrontation with Mangal Pandey and for his refusal to arrest Pandey even after being ordered to do so. As a punitive measure, the British authorities disbanded the entire 34th Bengal Native Infantry. A special court of inquiry established by the British East India Company concluded that Sikh and Muslim soldiers were more loyal and reliable, while Hindu soldiers, especially Brahmins, were deemed untrustworthy. Following this assessment, the British military began to reduce the number of Hindu recruits, particularly Brahmins, and increased enlistment from Sikh and Pathan communities.

EPILOGUE

'हम ने देखेंगे कल की बहारें तो क्या,
तुमको तो वो बहारें दिखा जाएँगे।'

*Though we may not live to see tomorrow's spring,
we will leave behind a world where it blooms for you.*

—*Shaheed* (1965)

India's struggle for independence is a saga of innumerable sacrifices—some remembered, many forgotten. The central purpose of this book is to remind the reader that standing trial was never easy; that life behind prison walls was never easy, especially when one did not know, when freedom itself appeared distant and uncertain. To offer one's life in the hope that even death might further ignite the cause of liberty was never easy either. To remain steadfast to one's ideals while making such a sacrifice demanded extraordinary courage, all the more so when there was no assurance that the sacrifice would ever be remembered.

Indian lawmakers, having themselves endured the British judicial system, understood that colonial criminal law functioned as an instrument of repression, cruelty and injustice against freedom fighters. In the immediate aftermath of Independence, reforms were introduced into the criminal justice system based on these lived experiences. Yet, the deeper remnants of colonial legal control endured for decades, finally being dismantled with the enactment of the new criminal laws in 2023: the Bharatiya Nyaya Sanhita (BNS), the Bharatiya Nagarik Suraksha Sanhita (BNSS), and the Bharatiya Sakshya Adhiniyam (BSA).

A stark illustration of colonial misuse of criminal law is found in the trial of Bhagat Singh, Sukhdev, Rajguru and others. When proceedings in the Lahore Conspiracy Case were perceived as moving too slowly, the then Viceroy Lord Irwin promulgated an ordinance in May 1930, transferring the trial to a Special Tribunal. This ordinance deprived the accused of their statutory right of appeal before the High Court under the CrPC and declared the Tribunal's decision final. It further empowered the Tribunal to continue the trial even in the absence of the accused. The unmistakable objective was to secure their execution at the earliest possible opportunity.

Examined through the lens of the present legal framework under the BNSS, the BNS, and the Constitution of India, such executive interference would be wholly impermissible today. The power to transfer criminal cases is no longer vested with the executive. Under Sections 446–448 of the BNSS, that authority lies exclusively with the judiciary. Likewise, Section 407 of the BNSS mandates that no death sentence passed by a Sessions Court may be executed without confirmation by the High Court, while Section 415 preserves the accused's right to appeal against a death sentence. These fundamental safeguards were expressly denied to Bhagat Singh and his co-accused by the colonial ordinance. The episode reveals a colonial legal mindset in which procedural fairness was subordinated to the imperative of securing convictions against Indian accused.

Another illustration of colonial bias emerges from the Kakori Conspiracy Case. There, Ram Prasad Bismil and the others accused raised a specific objection alleging bias on the part of the Committing Magistrate, Saiyid Ainuddin, on the grounds that he appeared as a witness in the very proceedings over which he presided. The Sessions Court noted that, in the ordinary course, the Magistrate's testimony ought to have been recorded for the first time before the Court of Session. Despite acknowledging that the course adopted by Saiyid Ainuddin—entering the witness box while simultaneously acting as Committing Magistrate—was highly unusual, the court rejected the objection.

Such a situation would be legally untenable today. Section 127 of the BSA expressly safeguards judicial impartiality by providing that no judge or magistrate shall, save under a special order of a superior court, be compelled to answer questions regarding their conduct or knowledge acquired in the discharge of judicial duties. This provision reinforces the separation between judicial functions and evidentiary roles, ensuring institutional neutrality in criminal trials.

The transition from colonial criminal law to the modern Indian criminal justice framework thus reflects a fundamental shift in purpose. While colonial law was designed to punish and suppress, contemporary criminal statutes are structured around fairness, due process and justice—values rooted in constitutional morality rather than imperial control.

The twelve trials chronicled in this book are narratives of the highest form of sacrifice made by India's freedom fighters. Their singular objective was to secure a better future for generations yet unborn—a future free from the chains of slavery. Whether it was Madan Lal Dhingra, Udham Singh, or Sachindra Nath Sanyal, each surrendered youth, comfort and ultimately life itself at the height of their prime, driven only by the hope that their actions would bring freedom to their country. In truth, it was not merely individuals who stood in the dock; it was freedom itself that was on trial.

Many lost their cases, and with them years of their lives—or life altogether. Yet freedom ultimately prevailed. The trysts with destiny made in the silence of solitary confinement, without any promise of redemption, were redeemed on 15 August 1947, even though those who made them were no longer alive to witness that dawn.

APPENDIX 1

PROCLAMATION OF THE PROVISIONAL GOVERNMENT OF AZAD HIND BY SUBHAS CHANDRA BOSE

After their first defeat at the hands of the British units 1757 in Bengal, the Indian people fought an uninterrupted series of hard and bitter battles over a stretch of one hundred years. The history of this period teems with examples of unparalleled heroism and self-sacrifice. And, in the pages of that history, the names of Siraj-Ud-Daulah and Mohan Lal of Bengal, Haider Ali, Tippu Sultan and Velu Tampi of South India, Appa Sahib Bhonsle & Peshwa Baji Rao of Maharashtra the Begums of Oudh, Sardar Shyam Singh, Atariwala of Punjab and last, but not least, Rani Laxmibai of Jhansi, Tantia Topi, Maharaj Kunwar Singh of Dumraon and Nana Sahib-among others the names of these warriors are forever engraved in letters of gold. Unfortunately for us, our forefathers did not at first realise that British constituted a grave threat to the whole of India and they did not therefore put up a united front against the enemy. Ultimately, when the Indian people were roused to the reality of the situation, they made a concerted move and under the flag of Bahadur Shah, in 1857 they fought their last war as free men. In spite of a series of brilliant victories in the early stages of this war, ill-luck and faulty leadership gradually brought about their final collapse and subjugation. Nevertheless, such heroes as the Rani of Jhansi, Tantia Topi, Kunwar Singh & Nana Sahib live like eternal stars in the nation's memory to inspire us to greater deeds of sacrifice and valour.

Forcibly disarmed by the British after 1857 and subjected to terror and brutality, the Indian people lay prostrate for a while but with the birth of Indian National Congress in 1885, there came a new awakening. From 1885 till the end of the last world war, the Indian people in their endeavour to recover their lost liberty, tried all possible methods, namely, agitation and propaganda, boycott of British goods, terrorism and sabotage and finally armed revolutions. But all these efforts failed for a time. Ultimately, in 1920, when the Indian people, haunted by a sense of failure, were groping for a new method, Mahatma Gandhi came forward with the new weapon of non-co-operation and civil disobedience.

For two decades thereafter, the Indian people went through a phase of intense patriotic activity. The message of freedom, was carried to every Indian home. Through personal example, people were taught to suffer, to sacrifice and to die in the cause of freedom. From the center to the remotest villages the people were knit together into one political organization. Thus, the Indian people not only recovered their political consciousness, but became a political entity, once again. They could now speak with one voice and strive with one will for one common goal. From 1937 to 1939, through the work of the Congress Ministries in eight Provinces, they gave proof of their readiness and their capacity to administer their own affairs.

Thus, on the eve of the present world war, the stage was set for the final struggle for India's liberation. During the course of this war, Germany, with the help of her allies, has dealt shattering blows to our enemy in Europe, while Nippon, with the help of her allies, has inflicted a knockout blow to our enemy in East Asia. Favoured by a most happy combinations of circumstances, the Indian people today have a wonderful opportunity for achieving their national emancipation.

For the first time in recent history, Indians abroad have also been politically roused and united in one organization. They are not only thinking and feeling in tune with their countrymen at home, but are also marching in step with them, along the path to Freedom. In East Asia, in particular, over two million Indians are now organized as one solid phalanx, inspired by the slogan of "Total Mobilization" and in front of them stand the serried ranks of India's Army of Liberation, with the slogan "Onward to Delhi", on their lips.

"Having goaded Indians to desperation by its hypocrisy and having driven them to starvation and death by plunder and loot, British rule in India has forfeited the goodwill of the Indian people altogether and is now living a precarious existence. It needs but a flame to destroy the last vestige of that unhappy role. To light that flame is the task of India's Army of Liberation. Assured of the, enthusiastic support of the civil population at home and also of a large section of Britain's Indian Army, and backed by gallant and invincible allies abroad but relaying in the first instance on its own strength, India's Army of Liberation is confident of fulfilling its historic role.

Now that the dawn of freedom is at hand, it is the duty of the Indian people to set up a Provisional Government of their own, and launch the last struggle under the banner of the Government. But with all the Indian leaders in prison and the people at home totally disarmed, it is not possible to set up a Provisional Government within India or to launch armed struggle under the aegis of that Government. It is therefore the duty of the Indian Independence League in East Asia, supported by all patriotic Indians at home and abroad, to undertake this task-the task of setting up a Provisional Government of Azad Hind (Free India) and of conducting the last fight for freedom, with the help of the Army of Liberation (that is, the Azad Hind Fauj or the Indian National Army) organized by the League.

Having been constituted as the Provisional Government of Azad Hind by the Indian Independence League in East Asia, we enter upon our duties with a full sense of the responsibility that has devolved on us. We pray that Providence may bless our work and our struggle for the emancipation of our Motherland. And we hereby pledge lives and the lives of our comrades in arms to the cause of her freedom, of her welfare and her exultation among the nations of the world.

It will be the task of the Provisional Government to launch and to conduct the struggle that will bring about the expulsion of the British and of their allies from the soil of India. It will then be the task of the Provisional Government to bring about the establishment of permanent National Government of Azad Hind constituted in accordance with the will of the Indian people and enjoying their confidence. After the British and their allies are overthrown and until a permanent National Government of Azad Hind is set up on Indian soil, the Provisional Government will administer the affairs of the country in trust for the Indian people.

The Provisional Government is entitled to, and hereby claims, the allegiance of every Indian. It guarantees religious liberty, as well as equal rights and equal opportunities to all its citizens. It declares its firm resolve to pursue the happiness and prosperity of the whole nation and of all its parts, cherishing all the children of the nation equally and transcending all the differences cunningly fostered by an alien government in the past.

In the name of God, in the name of bygone generations who have welded the Indian people into one nation and in the name of the dead heroes who have bequeathed to us a tradition of heroism and self-sacrifice, we call upon the Indian people to rally round our banner and to strike for India's Freedom. We call upon them to launch the final struggle against the British and all their allies in India and to prosecute that struggle with valor and perseverance and with full faith in final Victory-until the enemy is expelled from Indian soil and the Indian people are once again a Free Nation."

Signed on behalf of the Provisional Government of Azad Hind, Subhas Chandra Bose (Head of the State, Prime Minister and Minister for War and Foreign Affairs);

Capt. Mrs. Lakshmi (Women's organisation),
S. A. Ayar (Publicity and Propaganda);
Lt Col. A. C. Chatterjee (Finance);
Lt Col. Aziz Ahmed,
Lt Col. N. S. Bhagat,
Lt Col. J. K. Bhonsle,
Lt Col Gulzara Singh,
Lt Col. H.Z. Kiani,
Lt Col. A. D. Loganadan,
Lt Col. Ehsan Qadir.
Lt Col. Shah Nawaz (Representatives of the armed forces);

M. Sahay, Secretary (with ministerial rank);
Rash Bihari Bose (Supreme Adviser),
Karim Gani,
Debnath Das,
D. M. Khan,
A. Yellappa,
J. Thivy,

Sardar Ishar Singh (Adviser),
N. Sarkar (Legal Adviser),

Syonan,
October 21, 1943.

STATEMENT ON THE PROCLAMATION

As a student of history and in particular of revolutions in different parts of the world, during 22 years of public life, I always felt that what India was lacking in her fight for freedom were two things a National Army and a National Government to lead that army to battle. In the course of present war, thanks to the brilliant victories achieved by the armed forces of Nippon, it became possible for Indians in East Asia to organize the Indian Independence League and the Indian National Army.

The creation of a National Army gave reality and seriousness to the whole Independence Movement, in East Asia. If this Army had not been organized, the Independence League in East Asia would have been mere propaganda organ. With the creation of the National Army, it became possible, as well as necessary, to set up a Provisional Government of Azad Hind (Free India). The Government is born out of the Independence

League for the purpose of launching and directing the final struggle for India's freedom.

In setting up this Provisional Government, we are, on the one hand, meeting the exigencies of the Indian situation and are on the other, following in the foot-steps of history. In recent times the Irish people set up their Provisional Government in 1916. The Czechs, did the same during the last, world war. And, after the last world war the Turks under the Leadership of Mustapha Kemal, set up their Provisional Government in Anatolia. In our case, the Provisional Government of Azad Hind will be like the normal peacetime-Government. Its functions and its composition will be of a unique kind. It will be a fighting organization, the main object of which will be to launch and conduct the last war against the British and their allies in India. Consequently, only such departments will be run by the Government as will be necessary for the launching and the prosecution of the struggle for Liberty

The Cabinet will consist of a certain number who will represent the civil departments of the Government-while there will be others representing the Armed Forces of the Government. Since the purpose of the Government is to fight for Independence, the armed forces have been given a large representation on the Cabinet. Besides the ordinary Ministers of the Cabinet, provision has been made for a number of Advisers to the Cabinet. In this manner, the Provisional Government will maintain close and organic connection with the entire Indian community in East Asia and mobilize all their resources for the coming struggle. When the Provisional Government is transferred to Indian soil, it, will assume the functions of a normal government operating in its own territory. Many new departments will then be started. With the formation of a Provisional Government of Azad Hind, the Indian Independence Movement has obtained all the preconditions of success. It remains now to start the final struggle for freedom. This will begin when the Indian National Army crosses the frontier of India and commence its historic march to Delhi. This march will end only when the Anglo-American are expelled from India and the Indian National Flag is hoisted over the Viceroy's House in New Delhi.

APPENDIX 2

ARTICLES OF MAHATMA GANDHI PUBLISHED IN *YOUNG INDIA*

TAMPERING WITH LOYALTY

(Published on 19 September 1921)

His Excellency the Governor of Bombay had warned the public some time ago, that he 'meant business', that he was not going to tolerate the speeches that were being made. In his note on the Ali Brothers and others he has made clear his meaning. The Ali Brothers are to be charged with having tampered with the loyalty of the sepoy and with having uttered sedition. I must confess that I was not prepared for the revelation of such hopeless ignorance on the part of the Governor of Bombay. It is evident that he has not followed the course of Indian History during the past twelve months. He evidently does not know that the National Congress began to tamper with the loyalty of the sepoy in September last year, that the Central Khilafat Committee began it earlier still, for I must be permitted to take the credit or 'the odium of suggesting that India had a right openly to tell the sepoy and everyone who served the Government in any capacity whatsoever, that he participated in the wrongs done by the Government. The Conference at Karachi merely repeated the Congress declaration in terms of Islam, but speaking for Hinduism and speaking for nationalism I have no hesitation in saying that it is sinful for anyone, either as soldier or civilian, to serve this Government which has proved treacherous to the Mussalmans of India and which had been guilty of the inhumanities of the Punjab. I have said this from many a platform in the presence of sepoys. And if I have not asked individual sepoys to come out, it has not been due to want of will but of ability to support them. I have not hesitated to tell the sepoy that, if he could leave the service and support himself without the Congress or the Khilafat aid, he should leave at once. And I promise that, as soon as the spinning wheel finds an abiding place in every home and Indians begin to feel that weaving gives anybody any day an honorable livelihood, I shall not hesitate, at the peril of being shot, to ask the Indian sepoy individually to leave his service and become a weaver. For, has not the sepoy been, used to hold India under subjection, has he not been used to murder innocent people at Jallianwala Bagh, has he not been used to drive away innocent men, women and children during that dreadful night at Chandpur, has he not been used to subjugate the proud Arab of Mesopotamia, has he not been utilized to crush the Egyptians? How can any Indian having a spark of humanity in him and any Musselman having any pride in his religion feel otherwise than as the Ali Brothers have done? The sepoy has been used more often as a hired assassin than as a soldier defending the liberty or the honour of the weak and the helpless. The Governor has pandered to the basest in us by telling us what would have happened in Malabar but for the British soldier or sepoy.

Venture to inform His Excellency that Malabar Hindus would have fared better without the British bayonets, that Hindus and Mussalmans would have jointly appeased the Moplas, that possibly there being no Khilafat question there would have been no Moplas riot at all, that at the worst supposing that Mussalmans had common cause with the Moplas, Hinduism would have relied upon its creed of non-violence and turned every Musselman into a friend, or Hindu valour would have been tested and tried. The Governor of Bombay has done a disservice to himself and his cause (whatever it might be) by fomenting Hindu-Musselman disunion, and has insulted the Hindu as, by letting them infer from his note, that Hindus are helpless creatures unable to die for or defend their hearth, home or religion. If, however the Governor is right in his assumptions, the sooner the Hindus die out the better for humanity. But let me remind His Excellency that he has pronounced the greatest condemnation upon British rule, in that it finds Indians to-day devoid of enough manliness to defend themselves against looters, whether they are Mopla, Mussalmans or infuriated Hindus of Arrah.

His Excellency's reference to the sedition of Ali Brothers is only less pardonable than his reference to the tampering. For he must know that sedition has become the creed of the Congress. Every Non-cooperator is pledged to preach disaffection towards the Government established by law. Non-co-operation, though a religious and strictly moral movement, deliberately aims at the overthrow of the Government, and it is therefore legally seditious in terms of the Indian Penal Code. But this is no new discovery. Lord Chelmsford knew it. Lord Reading knows it. It is unthinkable that the Governor of Bombay does not know it. It was common cause that so long as the movement remained non-violent nothing would be done to interfere with it.

But it may be urged that the Government has a right to change its policy when it finds that the movement is really threatening its very existence as a system. I do not deny its right. I object to the Governor's note, because it is so worded as to let the unknowing public think that tampering with the loyalty of the sepoy and sedition were fresh crimes committed by the Ali Brothers and brought for the first time to His Excellency's notice.

However, the duty of the Congress and Khilafat workers is clear. We ask for no quarter; we expect none from the Government. We did not solicit the promise of immunity from prison so long as we remained non-violent. We may not now complain, if we are imprisoned for sedition. Therefore, our self-respect and our pledge require us to remain calm, unperturbed and non-violent. We have our appointed course to follow.

We must reiterate from a thousand platforms the formula of the Ali Brothers regarding the sepoys, and we must spread disaffection openly and systematically till it pleases the Government to arrest us. And this we do, not by way of angry retaliation, but because it is our Dharma. We must wear Khadi even as the brothers have worn it, and spread the Gospel of Swadeshi. The Mussalmans must collect for Smyrna Relief and the Angora Government. We must spread like the Ali Brothers the Gospel of Hindu-Muslim Unity and of non-violence for the purpose of attaining Swaraj and the redress of the Khilafat and the Punjab wrongs.

We have almost reached the crisis. It is well with a patient who survives a crisis. If on the one hand we remain firm as a rock in the presence of danger, and on the other observe the greatest self-restraint, we shall certainly attain our end this very year.

—M.K.G.

◆

A PUZZLE AND ITS SOLUTION

(Published on 15 December 1921)

Lord Reading is puzzled and perplexed. Speaking in reply to the addresses from the British Indian Association and the Bengal National Chamber of Commerce at Calcutta, His Excellency said: "I confess that when I contemplate the activities of a section of the community, I find myself still, notwithstanding persistent study ever since I have been in India, puzzled and perplexed. I ask myself what purpose is served by flagrant breaches of the law for the purpose of challenging the Government in order to compel arrest?" The answer was partly given by Pandit Motilal Nehru when he said on being arrested that he was being taken to the house of freedom. We seek arrest because the so-called freedom is slavery. We are challenging the might of this Government because we consider its activity to be wholly evil. We want to overthrow the Government. We want to compel its submission to the people's will. We desire to show that the Government exists to serve the people, not the people for Government. Free life under the Government has become intolerable, for the price exacted for the retention of freedom is unconscionably great. Whether we are one or many, we must refuse to purchase freedom at the cost of our self-respect or our cherished convictions. I have known even little children become unbending when an attempt has been made to cross their declared purpose, be it ever so flimsy in the estimation of their parents.

Lord Reading must clearly understand that the non-cooperators are at war with the Government. They have declared rebellion against it in as much as it has committed a breach of faith with the Mussalmans, it has humiliated the Punjab and it insists upon imposing its will upon the people and refuses to repair the breach and repent for the wrong done in the Punjab. There were two ways open to the people, the way of armed rebellion and the way of peaceful revolt. Non-cooperators have chosen, some out of weakness, some out of strength, the way of peace, i.e. voluntary Suffering.

If the people are behind the sufferers, the Government must yield or be overthrown. If the people are not with them, they have at least the satisfaction of not having sold their freedom. In an armed conflict the more violent is generally the victor. The way of peace and suffering is the quickest method of cultivating public opinion, and therefore when victory is attained it is for what the world regards as Truth. Bred in the atmosphere of law Courts, Lord Reading finds it difficult to appreciate the peaceful resistance to authority. His Excellency will learn by the time the conflict is over that there is a higher court than courts of justice and that is the court of conscience. It supersedes all other Courts.

Lord Reading is welcome to treat all the sufferers as lunatics, who do not know their own interest. He is entitled therefore to put them out of harm's way. It is an arrangement that entirely suits the lunatics and it is an ideal situation if it also suits the Government. He will have cause to complain if having courted imprisonment, non-cooperators fret and fume or 'whine for favours' as Lalaji puts it. The strength of a non-cooperator lies in his going to goals uncomplainingly. He loses his case if having courted imprisonment, he begins to grumble immediately his courtship is rewarded.

The threats used by His Excellency are unbecoming. This is a fight to the finish. It is a conflict between the reign of violence and of public opinion. Those who are fighting for the latter are determined to submit to any violence rather than surrender their opinion.

—M.K.G.

◆

SHAKING THE MANES

(Published on 23 February 1922)

How can there be any compromise whilst the British Lion continues to shake his gory claws in our faces? Lord Birkenhead reminds us that Britain has lost none of her hard fiber. Mr. Montagu tells us in the plainest language that the British are the most determined nation in the world, who will brook no interference with their purpose. Let me quote the exact words telegraphed by Reuter:

"If the existence of our Empire were challenged, the discharge of responsibilities of the British Government to India prevented and demands were made in the very mistaken belief that we contemplated retreat from India, then India would not challenge with success the most determined people in the world, who would once again answer the challenge with all the vigour and determination at its command."

Both Lord Birkenhead and Mr. Montagu little know that India is prepared for all the hard fibre that can be transported across the seas and that her challenge was issued in the September of 1920 at Calcutta that India would be satisfied with nothing less than Swaraj and full redress of the Khilafat and the Punjab wrongs. This does involve the existence of the Empire, and if the present custodians of the British Empire are not satisfied with its quiet transformation into a true Commonwealth of free nations, each with equal rights and each having the power to secede at will from an honorable and friendly partnership, all the determination and vigour of the most determined people in the world and the 'hard fibre' will have to be spent in India in a vain effort to crush the spirit that has risen and that will neither bend nor break. It is true that we have no 'hard fibre'. The rice-eating puny millions of India seem to have resolved upon achieving their own destiny without any further tutelage and without arms. In the Lokamanya's language it is their' 'birthright' and they will have it in spite of the 'hard fibre' and in spite of the vigour and determination with which it may be administered. India cannot and will not answer this insolence with insolence, but if she remains true to her pledge, her prayer to God to be delivered from such a scourge will certainly not go in vain. No empire intoxicated with red wine of power and plunder of weaker races has yet lived long in this world, and this British Empire, which is based upon organized exploitation of physically weaker races of the earth and upon a continuous exhibition of brute force, cannot live if there is a just God ruling the universe. Little do these so-called representatives of the British nation realise that India has already given many of her best men to be dealt with by the British 'hard fibre'.

Had Chauri Chaura not interrupted the even course of the national sacrifice, there would have been still greater and more delectable offerings placed before the Lion, but God had willed it otherwise. There is nothing, however, to prevent all those representatives in Downing Street and Whitehall from doing their worst. I am aware that I have written strongly about the insolent threat that has come from across the seas, but it is high time that the British people were made to realise that the fight that was commenced in 1920 is a fight to the finish, whether it lasts one month or one year or many months or many years, and whether the representatives of Britain re-enact all the indescribable orgies of the Mutiny days with redoubled force or whether they do not. I shall only hope and pray that God will give India sufficient humility and sufficient strength to remain non-violent to the end. Submission to the insolent challenges that are cabled out on due occasions is now an utter impossibility.

—M.K.G.

APPENDIX 3

ARTICLES PUBLISHED IN *KESARI* BY BAL GANGADHAR TILAK

THE COUNTRY'S MISFORTUNE

(Published on 12 May 1908)

No one will fail to feel uneasiness and sorrow on seeing that India, a country which by its very nature is mild and peace-loving, has begun to be in the condition of European Russia. Furthermore, it is indisputable that (the fact of) two innocent white ladies having fallen victims to a bomb at Muzaffarpur will specially inspire many with hatred against the people belonging to the party of rebels. That many occurrences of this kind have taken place in European Russia and are taking place even now, is a generally known historical fact. But we did not think that the political situation in India would, in such a short time, reach its present stage, at least that the obstinacy and perversity of the white official class (a) (bureaucracy) (a) of our country would (so soon) inspire with utter disappointment the young generation solicitous for the advancement of their country and impel them so soon to follow the rebellious path. But the dispensations of God are extraordinary (b). It does not appear from the statements of the persons arrested in connection with the bomb explosion case at Muzaffarpur, that the bomb was thrown through hatred (felt) for some individual or simply owing to the action of some badmash (c) madcap. Even Khudiram, the bomb-thrower, himself feels sorry that two innocent ladies of Mr. Kennedy's family fell victims (to it) in place of Mr. Kingsford: What, then, should be said of others? It is plain from the statements of those identical young gentlemen, who took this work in hand by founding a secret society, that they were fully aware that it was not possible to cause British rule to disappear from this country, by such monstrous deeds. None of the arrested persons have stated that the mere establishment of a secret society at the present time would do away with the oppressive official class. Some of the Anglo-Indian journalists have cast ridicule on these young men by insolently asking the question, "Will English rule disappear by the manufacture of a hundred muskets or ten or five bombs?" But we have to suggest to the said editors that this is not a subject for ridicule. The young Bengali gentlemen, who perpetrated those terrible things, do not belong to the class of thieves or badmashes (*c*); had that been so, as they would not also have made statements frankly to the Police, (as they have done) now. Though the secret society of the young generation of Bengal may have been formed like (that of) the Russian rebels for the secret assassination of the authorities, it plainly appears from their statements that it has been formed not for the sake of self-interest but owing to the exasperation produced by the autocratic exercise of power by the unrestrained and powerful white official class. It is known to all that the mutinies and revolts of the nihilists, that frequently occur even in Russia, take place for this very reason and, looking (at the matter) from this point of view, (one) is compelled to say that the same state of things, which has been brought about in Russia by the oppression of the official class composed of their own countrymen, has now been inaugurated in India in consequence of the oppression practiced by alien officers. There is none who is not aware that the might of the British Government is as vast and unlimited as that of the Russian Government. But rulers who exercise unrestricted power must always remember that there is also a limit to the patience of humanity. Since the partition of Bengal, the minds of the Bengalis have become most exasperated, and all their efforts to get the said partition canceled by lawful means (have) proved fruitless and it is known to the world that even Pandit Morley, or now Lord Morley, has given a flat refusal to their (request). Under these circumstances, no one in the world, except the white officials, inebriated with the insolence of authority, will think that not even a very few of the people of Bengal should become turn-headed and (d) feel inclined to commit excesses. Experience shows that even a cat shut up in a house rush with vehemence upon the person who confines (it there) and tries to kill him. That being the case, the Bengalis, no matter however powerless they might be thought to be, are human beings and should not the official class have remembered that, exactly like those of other men, the feelings of the Bengalis, (too), are liable to become fierce or mild as occasion demands? It is true that India having now been for many years under the sway of alien rulers, the fire, spirit or vehemence natural to the Indian people have to a great extent cooled down; but under no circumstances can this vehemence or indignation descend to zero degree and freeze altogether. Old or experienced leaders can, so far as they themselves are concerned, keep this indignation permanently within certain prescribed limits with the help of (their) experience or (mature) thought: but it is impossible for all the people of the country thus to keep their spirit, indignation or irritability always within such bounds; nay, it may even be said without hesitation that the inhabitants of that country in which it is possible for this feeling of indignation to always remain thus within prescribed bounds, are destined to remain perpetually in slavery. It is not that our rulers are not aware of this principle. English statesmen have settled the lines of British policy, fully bearing in mind that British rule in this country is alien and of the people of a different religious faith. When one country rules over another, the principal aim of the rulers is self-interest alone; but the extent of each self-interest is bounded in such a way that the subjects might not get exasperated. What is called statesmanship consists only in this; and this very thing has been designated (*a*) enlightened self-interest (*a*) by some English authors. British rule in India has been carried on this very principle, but the great mistake that is being committed in that (connection) is that the English official class does not at all take the advice or opinion of the subjects or their leaders in the matter of our administration. The whole contract of settling in what the welfare of the subjects consists and in what their loss consists has been taken by the white official class in their own hands. And they are vain enough to think in this wise-whatever thing we might do or whatever policy we might decide upon in (the light of) our wisdom or enlightened self-interest, must alone be uncomplainingly accepted as beneficial to themselves by the people of India and they must invoke a blessing upon us (for the same). But owing to the spread of Western education, it is not now possible for this condition to last (any longer). However enlightened the self-interest of the rulers might be, India must still be a loser thereby; and in order to prevent this loss, the power in the hands of the white official class must gradually come into our hands; there is no other alternative; such is now the view of many people in India and it is gaining ground. Such an impression being ultimately injurious to the ruling official class, the white official class here has become eager to suppress completely the writings, speeches or other means which produce that impression and if they had been able to drive the car of the entire administration solely according to their own views, many oppressive enactments like the Prevention of (Seditious) Meetings Act would by this time have been passed, and India would fully have become another Russia. But the experience gained from history, democratic public opinion in England and the awakening caused throughout the whole continent of Asia by the rise of an oriental nation like that of Japan have come in the way of the oppressive policy of our white official class and have imposed some restrictions on their imperial (autocratic) sway. However, the desire of the people gradually to obtain the rights of *Swarajya* (*c*) is growing stronger and stronger, and if they do not get rights by degrees, as desired by them, then some people at least out of the subject population, being filled with indignation or exasperation, will not fail to embark upon the commission of improper or horrible deeds recklessly. The Honorable Mr. Gokhale himself had, in the course of one of his speeches in the Supreme Legislative Council, given a hint of this very kind to our Government in the presence of the Viceroy and when Lala Lajpatrai was deported without trial and the proclamation (ordinance) about the prevention of meetings promulgated, other native editors of newspapers also had, like ourselves, plainly given the Government to understand that if they resorted in that manner to oppressive Russian methods (of administration), then the Indian subjects, too, would be compelled to imitate, partially at least, (the methods of) the Russian subjects! "As you sow, so you reap" is a well-known maxim. For rulers to tell their subjects, "We shall practice whatever oppression we like, deport anyone we choose without trial, partition any province we like, stop any meeting we choose, or prosecute anyone we like for sedition and send him to jail; (but) you, on your part, should silently endure all those things and should not allow your indignation, exasperation or vehemence to go beyond certain limits," is to show to the world that they do not know common human nature. Most of the Anglo-Indian newspaper editors have committed this very mistake when writing on the Muzaffarpur affair. They have brought a charge against the Indian leaders that it was by the very writings or speeches of the said leaders who passed severe comments on the high-handed or contumacious conduct of the English official class, that the present terrible situation was brought about; and they have next made a recommendation that Government should henceforth place greater restrictions upon the speeches, writings or movements of these leaders. In our opinion, this suggestion is most silly. Just as when a dam built across a river begins to give way owing to the flood caused by excessive rain, the blame for the (mishap) should be thrown on the rain and not on the flood, even so, if in society there is any transgression of legal bounds in a few cases owing to the discontent or exasperation engendered by the oppressive acts of an irresponsible and unrestrained official class, the blame or the responsibility for it must be placed on the policy of the unrestricted official class alone. Take any man you like; It is true that he does not see his real state. The crores of people, revolving round the earth's axis along with the earth itself, think that (it is) the world (that) is revolving and not themselves. Bat wise men should, instead of falling into such a delusion, find out the true reason of any particular thing and direct their attention to it. It is no use striking idly and continually a (piece of) rope after calling it a snake. The rule of the autocratic, unrestricted and irresponsible white official class in India is becoming more and more unbearable to the people. All thoughtful men in India are putting forth efforts in order that this rule or authority, instead of remaining with the said official class, should come into the hands of the representatives of the subject people. Some think that this thing can be accomplished by supplicating this intoxicated official class itself, or by petitioning the Government in England who exercise supervision over it. Some others think this improbable, and they have persuaded themselves into the notion that, in accordance with the maxim, the mouth does not open unless the nose is stopped, unless a spoke is put somewhere into (the wheels of) the car (of the administration) of the present rulers, their desired object will not be accomplished. The opinion of this party is that whatever may be wanted (by them) should be plainly stated and it should be obtained by (following) the path of (passive) resistance. But to say that not even a single man out of the thirty crores (of people) in the country should go beyond these two paths in the paroxysm of the indignation or exasperation produced by this oppressive system of Government, is like saying that the indignation or exasperation of the thirty crores of the inhabitants of India must always necessarily remain below a certain degree and it is impossible to fix such a limit for the whole country. Just as a man who cherishes a desire or makes an effort that when the sun in summer reaches the meridian the arid country in Maewar should remain as cool as Darjeeling or Shimla, must fail (to secure his object), similarly it is vain to entertain a desire or to make an effort that the indignation, exasperation or vehemence produced in the minds of the subjects by an unpopular system of administration should remain necessarily within a certain limit at all times and in all places. If there is any lesson to be learnt by our rulers from the Muzaffarpur bomb affair and from the statements of the young gentlemen implicated in it, it is this alone and we humbly take permission to bring this very thing again and again to their notice. We are aware that our government will, by assuming a stern aspect (and) by the adoption of harsh measures, be able to immediately stop outrages like the one that occurred at Muzaffarpur. But even if such means be necessary at the present time to maintain peace, still that will not completely remove the root of the disease, and so long as the disease in the body has not been rooted out, no one will be able to guarantee that if a boil in one part (of the body) is cut away, another will not develop again in some other part. It is the King's and the subjects' great misfortune that such times should befall a mild country like India which is naturally loyal and averse to horrible deeds. There is no difference of opinion that those who are responsible for the maintenance of peace in the country should immediately stop outrages of this kind on their coming to light but the remedies that are to be adopted with a view to prevent the repetition of such horrible calamities should only be adopted with foresight and consideration. It is now plain that not only has the system of Government in India become unpopular but also that the prayer made many times by the people for the reform of that system having been refused, even some educated people forgetting themselves in the heat of indignation have begun to embark upon the perpetration of improper deeds. Men of equal temperament and of reason in the nation will not approve of such violence; nay, there is even a possibility that in consequence of such violence increased oppression will be practiced upon the people for some time (to come) instead of its being stopped. But a glance at the recent history of Russia will show that such excesses or acts of violence are not at all stopped by subjecting the people to increased oppression. It is true that in order to acquire political rights efforts are required to be made for several successive generations and those efforts, too, are required to be made peacefully, steadily, persistently, and constitutionally! But while such efforts are being made, who will guarantee that no person whatsoever in society will go out of control? And as such guarantee cannot be given, how would it be reasonable to say that all persons who put forth efforts for acquiring political rights are seditious? This is what we do not understand. Just as it is difficult to lay down a restriction that not even a tear or two must fall from the eyes of a man while his heart has become sorely afflicted by sorrow in the same manner it is vain to expect that the unrestricted method of administration, under which India is being ruled over in a high-handed and reckless manner, should become only so far unbearable to the people that no one should become unduly exasperated and resort to excesses on that account. It may be said that, with the exception of some few individuals, the educated and uneducated classes in the country are not as yet prepared to transgress lawful or constitutional limits: nay, even such a desire has not risen in their minds. Under such circumstances to throw the responsibility of the horrible Muzaffarpur affair on that class is adding insult to injury. It cannot be that these things are not understood by a wise Government of the twentieth century, but the intoxication of unrestricted authority and the earnest desire to benefit one's own countrymen is so extraordinary that even wise men become blind thereby on certain occasions. The calamitous occasion which has befallen India at the present time is of this very kind. There is no possibility of the structure of British rule giving way in consequence of the murder of high white officers. If one passes away a second will come in his place, if the second passes away a third will succeed, there is no one whatever so foolish as not to understand this. But Government should take this lesson from the Muzaffarpur affair that the minds of some (persons) out of the young generation have begun to turn towards violence on seeing that all peaceful agitation for the acquisition of political rights has failed, just as a deer attacks a hunter, totally regardless of its own life, after all means of protection have been exhausted. No sensible man will approve of this excess or sinful deed. But it is impossible not only for the subjects but even for the King to avoid or to totally stop this traga (*f*) of desperation, and traga (*f*) really speaking is at all times the result only of a climax of exasperation and despair. True statesmanship, it may be said, consists, indeed in not allowing these things to reach such an extreme or (critical) stage, and this is the very policy we are candidly and plainly suggesting to Government on the present occasion. We do not think that we have done the whole of our duty as subjects by humbly informing

Government that the affair that occurred at Muzaffarpur was horrible and that we vehemently condemn or repudiate it. All heartily desire that such improper things should not take place and that none from amongst the subjects should have an occasion to resort to such extremes. But at such a time it must also be necessarily considered how far the ruling official class should, by utterly disregarding this desire of the subjects, try their patience to the uttermost; otherwise, it will not be possible to maintain cordial relations between the rulers and the subjects and to carry on smoothly the business of either. We have already said above that the Muzaffarpur affair was not proper (and) it was regrettable. But if the causes which give rise to it remain permanent in future exactly as they are at present, then in our opinion it is not possible that such terrible occurrences will stop altogether; and it is for this very reason that we have on this very occasion suggested to the Government the measures which should be adopted in order to put a stop altogether to such undesirable occurrences. The time has, through our misfortune, arrived when the party of * Nihilists, ' like that which has arisen in Russia, Germany, France and other countries, will now rise here. To avoid this contingency, to prevent the growth of this poisonous tree is altogether in the hands of Government. These abscesses affecting the country will never be permanently cured by oppression or by harsh measures. Reform of the administration is the only medicine to be administered internally for this disease; and if the official class does not make use of that medicine at this time, then it must be considered a great misfortune of all of us. The Government official class may perhaps dislike this writing of ours, but we cannot help it; for, as a poet has said, words both sweet and beneficial or hard to obtain. What we have said above is, in our opinion, true and reasonable and beneficial also to both the rulers and the subjects in the end. If in spite of this, our writing proves to be of no use, it must be considered a great misfortune of the country. What else? And when once a misfortune overtakes (one) who can tell what calamities will befall (him) in future? No one desires calamities or difficulties; but sometimes God does not leave it in our hands to avoid them. The present affair is becoming one of these sorts; and if the Government official class does not recognize this fact, what can we do? Our duty extends to the giving of a hint; and we are discharging that duty, remembering God and Truth. It is our desire also that the state of the country should not become distressful; but at the same time, we must also exercise the right which we have of insisting that the present intolerable system of administration should be reformed as soon as possible. It is no use being bewildered for nothing. We are aware that the white official class or the Anglo-Indian journalists will most astutely utilize Muzaffarpur affair to lessen the vehemence of our efforts; nay, their self-interest also lies in this. But it is our duty to strongly condemn also this perversion of the true state of things by Anglo-Indians, while condemning the desperate and suicidal deed perpetrated at Muzaffarpur. Just as it is the duty of the subjects to assist in preventing the murder of ruling officials, so also it is the duty of the rulers to admit (the voice of) public opinion into the administration (of the country) according to the present times, instead of keeping it (i.e. the administration) irresponsible. The scripture laying down the duties of kings is declaring at the top of its voice that it is not possible for the ruling individuals to forget this duty or to deliberately disregard it and to make the subjects only discharge their duties punctiliously; nay, (it further says that this) will be beneficial to neither party. Where this duty is disregarded, there the occurrence of calamities, some time or other, like that at Muzaffarpur is inevitable. Therefore, if the rulers wish that these undesirable incidents should not come to pass, our suggestion to them is that they should in the first instance impose restrictions upon their own system of administration itself, and it is only with that object in view that to-day's article has been written,

[His Imperial Majesty's High Court, Bombay,
Translator's Office, 2nd July 1908.]

A true Translation.

N.L. Manker,
Third Translator

◆

THESE REMEDIES ARE NOT LASTING

(Published on 9 June 1908)

From this week, the Government of India has again entered upon a new policy of repression. The fiend of repression has possession of the body of the Government of India after every five or ten years. The present occasion, too, is of this very kind. The Prevention of Meetings Act was passed, certainly after Lord Morley had become Secretary of State for India, and now an Act relating to newspapers has been passed. (The fact) that the fiends of repression should swarm everywhere while the Liberal party is in power and while a philosopher (and) an expounder of the principles of Liberalism like

(Mr.) Morley is holding the reins of administration, will make it evident to (our) readers how the Mantrikas (a) themselves have (b) abjured their ideals (b). What does a policy of repression mean? Repression means not only stopping future growth but nipping off past growth also. To stop the future progress of those causes which have given birth to the nation in India, which have developed the nation and which have created the national fire for the rise of the nation, and to drag those (causes) backwards by pulling them by the leg, is called a retrograde or repressive policy. Liberty of speech and liberty of the press give birth to a nation and nourish it. Seeing that these had begun to turn India into a nation, the official class had for many days entertained the desire to smash (c) both of them and they have gratified their ardent desire by taking advantage of the bomb in Bengal. Now the question arises, will this repressive policy bring about that which is in the mind of the official? The first desire of the official class is that bombs should be stopped in India, and that the mind of no one should feel inclined towards the manufacture or the throwing of bombs. That the authorities should entertain such a desire is natural and also laudable. But just as he who has to go towards the North goes to the South, or, he who is bound for the East takes the way to the West, in the same manner the authorities have taken a path leading to the very opposite direction (of their goal). This is exactly what is called infatuation. This aberration of the intellect suggests coming destruction; and seeing that the Government has adopted a repressive policy, (we) feel extremely grieved (to think) that more sorrowful days are henceforward (d) in store (d) for the subjects and the authorities. See how the understanding of the Government has become fatuous. The authorities have spread the false report that bombs of the Bengalis are subversive of society. There is as wide a difference between the bombs in Europe desiring to destroy society and the bombs in Bengal as between the earth and heaven. There is an excess of patriotism at the root of the bombs in Bengal, while the bombs in Europe are the product of the hatred felt for selfish millionaires (e). The Bengalis are not anarchists but they have brought into use the weapon of the anarchists: that is all. The anarchist murdering the President in Paris simply because he is the President, is one man; while the madcap patriot of Portugal throwing a bomb at the King of Portugal because he suppresses the Parliament is a different (person). The anarchist who murders a millionaire in America for the only reason that he is a millionaire is one man, while the exasperated Russian patriot who throws a bomb in despair because the Czar's officers do not grant the rights of the Duma in Russia, is different. No one should forget that the bombs in Bengal do not belong to the first category but to the second. The bomb in Portugal reflected a change in the system of government in Portugal and the ministry of the new boy-monarch had to abandon the previous repressive policy. The mightiest Czar of Russia, too, had the perforce to bow down before the bomb, and, while making repeated attempts to break up the Duma, was at last obliged to establish it as a matter of course. That the bombs came to a stop in Portugal, or, that the series of bombs in Russia did not lengthen will not be set down by anyone to the credit of the policy of repression. New desires and new ambitions have risen amongst the people and are gathering strength every day; such was the interpretation put upon bombs by the statesmen of both the aforesaid countries and accordingly they changed the character of the administration in such a way that the desires and the ambitions of the people should at least be partially gratified and that they should not become utterly desperate and resort to violence. The present repressive policy of the Government is of two sorts. First, the very manufacture of bombs is to be made impossible, and, secondly, such measures are to be taken that the people should not feel inclined at all to manufacture and throw bombs. After the parrot is first put into the cage, the door is closed. Accordingly, the Government first disarmed the people. In order that the caged parrot should feel delight only in remaining within the cage, people who are fond of pleasure and sport, make arrangements for (providing it there with) sweet fruits and grain and water. But the Indian Government has not only closed the door of the cage, but it has also commenced to pluck the wings and break the leg (of the parrot) in order that it should not go out (of the cage)! Even the tyrannical rulers of Europe did not disarm their subjects even a savage race like the Mussalmans did not disarm the Hindus while exercising their imperial sway over India. Then, why did the English do so? If common muskets and common swords are in the hands of the subjects, they can never equal the military strength (of Government). If there is nothing detrimental to the military strength (of Government) even in allowing the people to be with arms, then why did the English commit the great sin of castrating a nation? The answer to this question is that the manhood of the nation was slain by the Arms Act in order that the authority exercised even by petty officials from day to day should be unopposed and that the selfish administration might be carried on all right without any hitch (and) without granting the subjects any of the rights of *Swarajya!* The English have not got even as much generosity as the Moghuls and they have not even as much military strength as the Moghuls. As compared with the imperial sway of the Moghuls, the English Empire in India is extremely weak and wanting in vigor from the point view of military strength. The Emperor Aurungzeb exercised tyranny of various kinds over the Hindus from the point of view of religion though not from the point of view of the distribution of wealth and his ten or twenty lakhs of troops also perished completely during his Deccan campaigns of ten or twenty years. Still the Empire of Delhi lasted for a hundred and fifty years, albert in a hobbling manner, after his death. If the English army in India were to be confronted by difficulties similar to those which Aurungzeb's forces encountered, then the English rule will not last in India even for, quarter of a century after (that). The principal reason for this is that the English remain in India like temporary (*f*) tenants or mere (*g*) birds of passage (*g*). The residence of the English in India not being permanent, and the English authorities as well as the English merchants having a covert aim at enriching England, they are, quite naturally, not ready to give into the hands of the natives any portion of the ruling power after making a separate division (of the same). Had the Moghuls exercised (their) imperial sway over India, for the sake of the prosperity of the land of their original residence, by sending out officers like temporary tenants, then the Moghuls, too would have been obliged to be illiberal in dealing with Princes and Chiefs or village institutions, like the English themselves, and there would have been no other alternative but to disarm the subjects. Owing to the power given by Western science and the helplessness produced amongst the subjects in consequence of their being disarmed, the administration can be heedlessly carried on without any hitch (and) without even a consideration of the desires or the aspirations of the people. Owing to the bomb this state (of things) has not remained permanent. The subjects, armless; and the Government, admittedly powerful owing to the modern science of arms. Up to this time there was no means at all for the Government to know (h) that the people becoming disappointed owing to some acts of Government, get exasperated and become even turn-headed. How was the Government at all to know that the tyranny of its acts had become unbearable to the subjects? What happened usually up to this time when Government did any act and the subjects disapproved of it? The people used to submit petitions, to prefer requests; the authorities used to say that it was a temporary froth, that it would subside, in a short time, of itself. The people become despondent, the impatient fretted and fumed within themselves in exasperation, and the turn-headed, in their own violent emotion, burnt their bodies and in a fit of passion made an offering of themselves alone, -without even any report of any kind reaching the ears of Government; such was the state (of things) up to this time. The turn-headed men destitute of arms became provided with arms in consequence of the bomb, and the bomb reduced the importance (*i*) of military strength. Unless a beginning be made to divide wealth and authority with the subject, with greater liberality than was shown by the Moghuls, England will not henceforward be able to carry on the administration, without any hitch, through officers having (only) a temporary (interest in the country). The bomb is not a thing like muskets or guns. Muskets and guns may be taken away from the subjects by means of the Arms Act; and the manufacture, too, of guns and muskets without the permission of Government, may be stopped; but is it possible to stop or to do away with the bomb by means of laws or the supervision of officials or the busy swarming of the detective police? The bomb has more the form of knowledge, it is a (kind of) witchcraft, it is a charm, an amulet. It has not much the features of a visible object manufactured in a big factory. Big factories are necessary for the bombs required by the military forces of the Government, but not much (in the way of) materials is necessary to prepare five or ten bombs required by violent, turn-headed persons. Virendra's big factory of bombs consisted (*j*) of one or two jars and five or ten bottles; and Government chemical experts are at present disposing that the factory was, from a scientific point of view, faultless like a government bomb-factory. Should not the Government pay attention to the true meaning of the accounts published in (the course of) the case of Virendra's conspiracy? Judging from the accounts published of this case, the formula of the bomb does not at all appear to be a lengthy one and (its) process also is very short indeed. The power of keeping the knowledge of this formula a secret from one who is turn- headed, has not now been left in the laws of Government. This knowledge is not a secret in Europe, America, Japan and other countries. In India it is still a secret knowledge. But when the number of turn-headed (persons) increases owing to the stringent enforcement of the policy of repression, what time will it take for the magical practices, the magical lore of Bengal to spread throughout India? The labour of acquiring this lore will not be as hard to those who are turn-headed as the labour of bringing their brains again to a normal condition, and even in putting this lore to a practical use there is very little possibility of the exasperation being even calmed down through a Magistrate, owing (to the plot) being frustrated by the skill and vigilance of the detective police. To speak in (the language of hyperbole, this factory can be brought into existence in a trice and (also) broken up in a trice! Therefore, how can the nose-string of the law be put on these turn-headed wizards when the Explosives (k) Act was passed in England (about) ten or fifteen years ago, the bomb had not attained such a form of knowledge (as at present). The bomb had not (then) become a (*l*) mere toy (*l*) of the Western sciences. At that time elaborate(m) appliances, too, were required; also, special materials were required and the factory also used to be a big one. Such things can be prevented by law, but when science begins to exhibit wonders like the bomb in mere sport (and even) while walking, talking (and) sleeping, how can these simple sports of science be put to a stop? The Westerners propitiated the goddess of science for (securing) commercial progress and military strength. How will it be to accept only the gift of the blessing of the propitiated goddess and to refuse only those things which that very goddess may be doing in mere sport in order that no one may become intoxicated with the bestowal of the blessings? While the knowledge of science of the westerners is being thus easily obtained (by people) every day, and while new discoveries are being made daily that produce terrific powers in no time with a simple process from common chemicals themselves which are constantly required for trade and industries, how long will the Government stop, by legal restraints, the current sport of scientific experts? In our opinion, Governments are going to put themselves and the subjects to loss for nothing, by pursuing impossible things. If the perfect state to which scientific knowledge has attained in Europe and America be considered, (one) has to say that the Government has been engaged in the vain attempt of making an impossibility a possibility. At such (a) time (as) this, chemists, persons engaged in industries and petty manufacturers cannot fail to be subjected to unjust compulsion for nothing. The object desired by the Government cannot be accomplished by the Explosives Act, but, on the other hand, it will serve as an instrument in the hands of the police and the petty officials to persecute good men. This effort to impose (*n*) a Prohibition (*n*) upon the scientific knowledge about bombs and the materials (for making bombs) is vain. If bombs are to be stopped this is not the proper means (for it); Government should act in such a way that no turn-headed man should feel any necessity at all for (throwing) bombs. When do people who are engaged in political agitation become turn- headed? It is when young (political) agitators feel keen disappointment (by being convinced) that their faculties, their strength and their self-sacrifice cannot be of any use in bringing about the welfare of their country in any other way than by acts of turn-headedness, that they become turn-headed. Government should never allow keen disappointment (to take hold) of (the minds of) those intelligent persons who have been awakened (to the necessity of) securing the rights of Swarajya. The government should not forget that when the desires and aspirations of the awakened intelligent people spread throughout the nation and begin rudely to awaken the whole nation, the disappointment instead of decreasing becomes all the keener, if this process of awakening is stopped at such a time. Government has passed the new 'Newspapers' Act with a view to put a stop to the process of awakening; and, therefore, there is a possibility of disappointment assuming a more terrible form and of turn headedness being produced even amongst people of thoughtful and quiet disposition. The real and lasting means of stopping bombs consists in making a beginning to grant the important rights of Swarajya (to the people). It is not possible for measures of repression to have a lasting (effect) in the present condition of the Western sciences and that of the people of India.

[H. I. M.'s High Court. Bombay,
Translator's Office, 7 July 1908]

APPENDIX 4

POSTER THROWN IN THE ASSEMBLY HALL BY BHAGAT SINGH AND BATUKESHWAR DUTT

It takes a loud voice to make the deaf hear, with these immortal words uttered on a similar occasion by Valliant, a French anarchist martyr, do we strongly justify this action of ours.

Without repeating the humiliating history of the past ten years of the working of the Reforms (Montague-Chelmsford Reforms) and without mentioning the insults hurled at the Indian nation through this House the so-called Indian Parliament- we want to point out that, while the people are expecting some more crumbs of reforms from the Simon Commission, and are ever quarrelling over the distribution of the expected bones, the Government is thrusting upon us new repressive measures like the Public Safety and the Trade Disputes Bill, while reserving the Press Sedition Bill for the next session. The indiscriminate arrests of labour leaders working in the open field clearly indicate whither the wind blows.

In these extremely provocative circumstances, the Hindustan Socialist Republican Association, in all seriousness, realizing their full responsibility, had decided and ordered its army to do this particular action, so that a stop be put to this humiliating farce and to let the alien bureaucratic exploiters do what they wish, but they must be made to come before the public eye in their naked form.

Let the representatives of the people return to their constituencies and prepare the masses for the coming revolution, and let the Government know that while protesting against the Public Safety and Trade Disputes Bills and the callous murder of Lala Lajpat Rai, on behalf of the helpless Indian masses, we want to emphasize the lesson often repeated by history, that it is easy to kill individuals but you cannot kill the ideas. Great empires crumbled while the ideas survived Bourbons and Czars fell, while the revolution marched ahead triumphantly.

We are sorry to admit that we who attach so great a sanctity to human life, we who dream of a glorious future, when man will be enjoying perfect peace and full liberty, have been forced to shed human blood. But the sacrifice of individuals at the altar of the 'Great Revolution' that will bring freedom to all, rendering the exploitation of man by man impossible, is inevitable.

Long Live the Revolution

Sd/ Balraj[*]

Commander-in-Chief

[*]The name 'Balraj' was famously used as an alias by the Indian revolutionary Chandra Shekhar Azad, who used to sign pamphlets as the commander-in-chief of the Hindustan Socialist Republican Army (HSRA)

APPENDIX 5

THE REVOLUTIONARY PAMPHLET (MANIFESTO OF HRA) PUBLISHED BY RAM PRASAD BISMIL

"Chaos is necessary to the birth of a new star" and the birth of life is accompanied by agony and pain. India is also taking a new birth and is passing through that inevitable phase, when chaos and agony shall play their destined role, when all calculations shall prove futile, when the wise and the mighty shall be bewildered by the simple and the week, when great empires shall crumble down and new nations shall arise and surprise humanity with the splendour and glory which shall be all its own.

This new power, which is shaking the world from its very depths, this new spirit which is working miracles behind the scene, is also manifesting itself in the young blood of India and is taking the shape of a movement which is despised and ignored by the wise and the learned, and is being described as the wild dreams of a few mad men. This remarkable movement is the revolutionary movement in young India.

The revolutionary movement has unnerved the weak, has inspired the robust and healthy, and has confounded the worldly wise and the learned. This movement can never be crushed just as much as the coming of the spring can never be thwarted. It will never die out until it has fulfilled the mission for which it has taken its birth.

Tyrants will oppress it, the faithless will taunt at it, and the confounded will denounce it, but thoughts and ideas can never be crushed by the sword, and the noble impulse that has taken birth in the very depths of out being can never be ignored, nor taunted.

This revolutionary movement is the manifestation of the new life that has taken birth in the Nation. To denounce this life is to denounce one's own understanding.

Twenty years of ruthless repression has not been able to crush it. Scathing denunciation by the renowned public leaders has not been able to arrest its steady growth. The movement stands mightier today than what it was before. The prospects of this revolutionary party were never so bright as they are today. This future is assured. Let no Indian deny the existence of this revolutionary party in order to denounce the repressive measures of the foreign rulers. The foreigners have no right to rule over India and therefore they must be denounced and driven out. Not that they have committed any particular act of violence or crime. There are the natural consequences of a foreign rule. This foreign rule must be abolished. They have no justification to rule over India except the justification of sword and therefore the revolutionary party had taken to the sword. But the sword of the revolutionary party bears ideas at its edge.

The immediate object of the revolutionary party in the domain of politics has been to establish a federal United Republics of India by an organized and armed revolution.

The final constitution of this Republic shall be framed and declared at a time when the representatives of India shall have the power to carry out their decision. But the basic principles of this Republic will be universal suffrage and abolition of all system which make the exploitation of man by man possible, e.g. the railways and other means of transportation and communication, the mines and other kinds of very great industries such as the manufacture of steel and ships all these shall be nationalized. In this Republic the electors shall have the right to recall their representatives, if so desired, otherwise the democracy shall become a mockery. In this Republic, the legislature shall have the power to control the executives and replace them whenever necessity will arise.

The revolutionary party is not national but international in the sense that its ultimate object is to bring harmony in the world by respecting and guaranteeing the diverse interests of the different nations. It aims not at cooperation between the different nations and states and in this respect, it follows the footsteps of great Indian Rishis of the glorious past and of Syndicalist France in the modern age. Good for humanity is no vain and empty word with the Indian revolutionaries. But the weak, the coward and the powerless can do no good either to themselves or to humanity.

With regard to the communal question, the revolutionary party contemplates to grant whatever rights the different communities may demand, provided they do not clash with the interests of other communities and they lead ultimately to hearty and organic union in different communities in the near future.

In the domain of economic and social welfare the party will foster the spirit of cooperation on as large a scale as possible.

Instead of private and unorganized business enterprises, the party prefers cooperative union. In the spiritual domain the party aims at establishing the truth and preaching it that the world in not Maya, an illusion to be ignored and despised at, but that it is the manifestation of the one individual soul, the supreme source of all power, all knowledge and all beauty. The revolutionary party has its own policy and its own programme. It cannot for obvious reasons divulge all its secrets. But when it will become quite sure that the government happens to know more than our own people, then the public will also be informed of its plan and methods without any hesitation at will. This revolutionary party pursues the policy of cooperation when possible and dissociation where necessary with the Indian National Congress and its different parties. But this party views all constitutional agitation in this country with contempt and ridicule. It is a mockery to say that India's salvation can be achieved through constitutional means, where no constitution exists. It is a self-deception to say that India's political liberty can be attained through peaceful and legitimate means. When the enemy is determined to break the peace at his own convenience, the fine phrase "legitimate" loses all its charm and significance when one pledges himself to maintain peace at all costs. Our public leaders hesitate to speak in plain terms that India wants complete autonomy free from foreign control. They perhaps are ignorant of the fact that nations are born through the inspiration of great ideals. The spiritual ideal which hesitates to accept the spirit of complete autonomy can hardly be called spiritual, though it may seemingly appear the most unmistakable terms and to place before the nation an ideal worth the name.

The ideal before us is to serve humanity in an organized

way. The ideal can never be realised by India so long as India remains British India. In order that India may realise her ideal she must have a separate and independent existence. This independence can never be achieved through peaceful and constitutional means. Even a child can understand that the laws that govern British India are not made by Indians, nor can they have any control over them. British India can never be transformed into a federal republic of the United Republics of India through the British laws and constitution. Young Indians! Shake off your illusion, face realities with a stout heart, and do not avoid struggle, difficulties and sacrifices. The inevitable is to come. Do not be misguided any more. Peace and tranquility you cannot achieve by peaceful and legitimate means. The following memorable words of a great English author Mr. Robertson may serve to make the wise men of India wiser still:

"The movement and programme of reform was mainly the achievement of Irish and Protestant leaders, to whom British statement had revealed the fatal secret that England could be bullied but not argued into justice and generosity."

—English Under Hanoverians, page-197

Indian public leaders are still ignorant of this fatal secret, or else they are foolishly wise to remain ignorant.

The wise men of India say that it is absurd to cherish the hope that India can be reconquered by force of arms, though they forget that it is equally or more absurd to believe that a handful of Englishmen have kept under subjugation by the force of arms, though they forget that it is equally or more absurd to believe that a handful of Englishmen have kept under subjugation by the force of arms one-fifth of the whole human race. Posterity may well doubt the authenticity of this fact that a handful of Englishmen even ruled over India for a century; it is so inconceivable. A few words more about terrorism and anarchism. These two words are playing the most mischievous part in India today. They are being invariably misapplied whenever any reference to revolution arises to be made, because it is so very convenient to denounce the revolutionary under that name. The Indian revolutionaries are neither terrorists nor anarchists. They never aim at spreading anarchy in the land and therefore they can never properly be called anarchists. Terrorism is never their object and they cannot be called terrorists. They do not believe that terrorism alone can bring independence and they do not want terrorism for terrorism's sake although they may at times resort to this method as a very effective means of retaliation. The present government exists simply because the Foreigners have successfully been able to terrorise the Indian people. The Indian people do not love their English masters, they do not want them to be here; but they do help the Britishers simply because they are terribly afraid of them and this very fear resists the Indians from extending their helping hands to the revolutionaries, not that they do not love them. The official terrorism is surely to be met by counter-terrorism. A spirit of utter helplessness pervades every strata of our society and terrorism is an effective means of restoring the proper spirits in the society without which progress will be difficult. Moreover, the English masters and their hired lackeys can never be allowed to do whatever they like, uninterrupted, unmodested. Every possible difficulty and resistance must be thrown in their way. Terrorism has an international bearing also, because the ardent enemies of England are at once drawn towards

Indian through terrorism and revolutionary demonstrations, and the revolutionary party has deliberately abstained itself from entering into this terroristic campaign at the present movement even at the greatest of provocations in the form of outrages committed on their sisters and mothers by the agents of a foreign government, simply because the party is waiting to deliver the final blow. But when expediency will demand it, the party will unhesitatingly enter into a desperate campaign of terrorism, when the life of every official and individual who will be helping the foreign ruler in any way will be made intolerable, be he Indian or European, high or low. But even then, the party will never forget that terrorism is not the object, and they will try incessantly to organize a band of selfless and devoted workers who will devote their best energies towards the political and social emancipation of their country. They will always remember that the making of nations requires the self-sacrifice of thousands of obscure men and women who care more for the idea of their country than for their own comfort or interest, their own lives or the lives of those whom they love.

Vijay Kumar*
President, Central Council

*The name 'Vijay Kumar' was famously used as an alias by the Indian revolutionary Ram Prasad Bismil, who used to sign pamphlets published by the Hindustan Republican Army (HRA).

ACKNOWLEDGEMENTS

In 2022, I was honoured to meet Shri Ashok Mehta, former Additional Solicitor General and a respected senior advocate, at a meeting in Bangalore. It was there that he first shared the idea of writing a book on the famous pre-Independence trials that played a significant role in shaping India's freedom struggle. From that day, the idea stayed with me, quietly growing in my mind.

When I finally began working on it in the winter of 2024, I quickly realized that this would not be an easy task. Many of the original trial records were difficult to access, and sourcing authentic material proved challenging. There was a point when I almost gave up, as my professional commitments as a lawyer were increasing and I found myself unable to devote enough time to my family. But, as the saying goes, 'Hoi Vahi Jo Ram Rachi Rakha'—what is destined shall happen. Somehow, I managed to find time amidst my professional obligations, family responsibilities and my duties as Secretary of the Adhivakta Parishad, Delhi Prant.

I will always remain deeply grateful to Mehta Sir for planting this idea in my mind and inspiring me to bring it to life. I would also like to acknowledge the valuable contributions of Shri Vikramjeet Banerjee, Additional Solicitor General, Supreme Court of India, and Shri Sanjoy Ghose, Senior Advocate, both of whom provided insightful feedback after reviewing the first draft of the book.

I express my deepest gratitude to Shri Shreehari Borikar ji, organizing secretary, Akhil Bhartiya Adhivakta Parishad, for his constant encouragement and unwavering motivation. His faith in this work, even in its earliest and most uncertain stages, was a source of strength and clarity. This book owes much to his guidance and generosity of spirit.

My sincere thanks also goes to Professor Seema Singh, Campus Law Centre, University of Delhi, for taking time out of her busy schedule to review the draft and offer her thoughtful suggestions. I am thankful to Ms Aarushi Bajpai, Associate Professor, Jindal Global Law School, and her exceptionally talented husband Mr Akash Gupta, Associate Professor, Jindal Global Law School, for sharing their valuable inputs and encouragement.

Finally, my heartfelt gratitude goes to my wife Pallavi Awasthi—also a practising advocate—and my beautiful daughters, Aashvi Vajpai and Kashvi Vajpai, without whose constant love, patience and support this book would never have been possible. The time that rightfully belonged to them was instead spent on the pages of this work. This book exists because of their understanding and strength.

I hope readers find it worth the time and effort that went into its writing.